The
L✓VE
LIST

THE LOVE LIST: FAST TRACK TO FOREVER

2025 fEMPOWER Press Trade Paperback Edition
Copyright © 2025 Celeste Pennington & Dave Pennington

Published in Canada, for Global Distribution by fEMPOWER Publications
www.fempower.pub | For more information email: media@fempower.pub

ISBN trade paperback: 978-1-998721-26-9
Ebook: 978-1-998721-27-6

To order additional copies of this book: media@fempower.pub

The LOVE LIST

CELESTE PENNINGTON
AND DAVE PENNINGTON

TO ALL THOSE WHO KEEP
THEIR HEARTS OPEN, EVEN AFTER
THEY'VE BEEN HURT

CHAPTER 1 – CELESTE
DECEMBER 2008

We pull through the ferry gate and into our designated lane. As soon as I turn off my car, Mike jumps out, but I stay buckled in, lost in thought with memories flooding back. This seems to be happening a lot lately.

I was born on the island but moved to the interior when I was young, and we settled in the Okanagan Valley. It was a beautiful place to live and grow up—dry rolling sage-colored hills in hot sunshine that framed the edges of the valleys lined with vineyards, orchards, and glistening lakes everywhere you looked. Seasons that smelled of slow ripening peaches, cherries, and apples. Our neighborhood was at one end of a magical lake: deep blue in the middle, the most vibrant shade of turquoise at the edges. It still takes my breath away.

I was new to the area when I started high school, yet it only took a few weeks to feel like I belonged. I quickly found a strong core group of people who accepted me immediately, and from then on, it was about having fun and making memories. Most weekends were spent walking around our area, spending time on friends' boats, and making plans for that night. *Who's hosting the party? Or will we have a huge bonfire out at one of the logging roads?* Even before we got our driver's licenses, we all felt independent. Most of our parents didn't really care where we were as long as we were with friends, because our town was small and felt safe. It was quite rural, ripe with

1

farming and fruit stands showcasing the riches that came from the lush landscape. We felt fortunate to be able to experience what the beautiful Okanagan Valley had to offer.

We had five years together, building ourselves up and cheering each other on. No one had to be part of a particular "club" to be friends. The jocks, the brains, the drama kids, the preppy crowd, and the smokers all mingled, and my friendship group was made up of them all. Labels didn't keep us apart. And once we started turning sixteen, almost everyone had access to a car. It was never anything fancy; all we cared about was a set of wheels. We didn't have our own phones back then, so school was where we made plans, including who would be the designated driver.

I have some incredible memories with my best friend, Dallas. Her family lived on a large piece of acreage in a stunning two-story farmhouse on the outskirts of town. Her mom would usually drive us wherever we wanted to go in those early years, but on the nights we knew we wanted to drink, we would sneak whatever we could get our hands on and pour it into an old shampoo bottle, then walk it down the driveway in the daytime: ten fence posts down and ten steps into the hayfield. Later, when our friends came to pick us up, we would grab it on our way out. I spent so many years at their house, being looked after like one of their own. We'd spend hours in Dallas's pink girly bedroom, getting ready in front of her vanity and deciding what outfit would look best. A Club Monaco sweatshirt and white jeans was my go-to.

In those years, it seemed like anything was possible, probably because it was. Living where we did brought endless options, so even in the winter we would snowboard in the local mountains. For my grade eleven year, I participated in an outdoor education program for half the year, and that experience was a huge part of me growing into myself. I began learning what I was capable of, and saying yes to new experiences was always the way to go. The classroom itself was outside, and we rode our bikes to and from the program. We learned how to sleep outside without supplies, how to start a fire, how to make shelter and track animals. We made baskets out of cider roots and designed and created native beading art. But the best part was the trips we prepared for and then experienced: ocean kayaking in the Gulf Islands and hiking and sleeping in the snow-covered Cathedral Mountains; being flown by helicopter up into the Rocky Mountains to a remote cabin where we then did day trips heli-skiing, careful not to start an avalanche. These people became family just as much as my friends who were not in the program. Even our graduation was an epic three days of whitewater rafting with the entire grade. We had fundraised all year and did so well that we almost paid for every students' whole trip. But everything I learned about nature couldn't compare to what I learned about myself.

I turned into such a tenacious, bold, happy, outspoken, smart, kind person. I felt like the world was in my hands, that anything was possible, and that I could do whatever I wanted for the rest of my life. Nothing was going to get in my way, because I was at the helm, driving my own crazy bus into every opportunity and possibility that came my way.

As I sat waiting for the ferry and reflecting on my past, I could see it was like a classic John Hughes movie, except it was real and it was my life. So, when did life start to feel so gray, with the odd splash of black and white? Where did the technicolor go?

My life has become mundane, so lifeless, so settled. To be honest, I don't even remember what it feels like to live with that kind of optimism and hope. How had I gotten here? My life in the Okanagan was so bright and promising, and I took that attitude with me when I left for

Vancouver. But soon after, I could only feel the rain of the coast, not the sunshine of the mountains.

I look out the window and sigh and think about driving to the island with Mike to spend Christmas with his family.

Unlike me, Mike was born and raised in one house, so when we visit, we actually stay in his childhood bedroom. And if I'm being honest, I am envious of the feeling of normalcy that comes with something so simple. Having the same bedroom to come home to year after year and at every holiday that follows, even though it is through proxy, instills a feeling in me of safety and routine by knowing I will always see the same things, the same bed, the same duvet, the same posters.

We have been together just over eight years, and while it hasn't always been an easy ride, it has been one I have committed to in my heart. I met Mike shortly after my arrival in Vancouver, and I fell for him in a blink.

Over the years, the promise of marriage was thick in the air with every celebration, like a smell that swallowed up all my thoughts every time it looked like there was an opportunity for him to get down on one knee. But it didn't happen on the family trip to Mexico. It didn't happen on my thirtieth birthday when all our friends and family were there, nor in those moments when it was just the two of us watching the sunset at Kits Beach. We've lived on and off together for five years. That has to mean something, right? Turning thirty had me feeling a little more secure in myself and ready to step into "adulthood." But at thirty-one, my patience was becoming more strained. I was ready for marriage and to start a family.

I've always been a people pleaser. It's in my nature to put others first. This was especially true after my parents' divorce when I would do anything to be seen and loved. So, even though Mike has always been a step behind me when it comes to our commitment, living together and sharing our lives has been enough for me. His family treats me like a daughter and thinks I will always be around, especially as I haven't left yet.

We all privately think the same thing: Mike will grow up one day and commit. I am sticking it out and waiting for him to mature, putting his needs before my own. I supported him when he wanted to try some career changes and was his biggest fan while he made documentaries. I mothered him through a health crisis, ensuring he got whatever he needed. I commiserated with him as he complained about how unjust it was that he had to change his diet, and I did whatever I could to make the transition as painless as possible.

We have been through a lot, but I am starting to feel that those years were always about his well-being, and no matter how much I've tried to make things work, I have never felt worse or so low. I wonder if my focus on him has resulted in me forgetting about myself. Maybe when you tell yourself enough times this is it and time passes, you feel like it's too late to start over. You accept whatever you're given and convince yourself that a proposal would solve it all and you'll finally feel happy and secure.

I open the windows a crack and smell the salty air. The sun is peeking out through the clouds and there is mist rising in the air from the latest downpour of rain. I feel the sudden urge to get my thoughts out of my head, so I reach into the back seat and get my journal out of my backpack. I have no idea why I have it with me. I was forever the girl who loved to buy journals, but I only ever wrote in the first couple pages, after which the journal joined the rest of the beautiful rainbow pile of empty pages. I'm not sure what is different today, but I'm feeling a shift inside, like a yearning for change, so I open the first page of the journal and wonder what to write about. Our relationship has been heavy on my mind lately, like we are at a turning point, and then a thought occurs about a recent magazine article that had been at the lunch table at work: "Make a List of Everything You Want in a Partner."

Why not write out all the reasons why Mike is my true love? So, pen to paper, I start writing what matters most to me in a partner.

It actually doesn't take much thinking, and my pen sails over the paper, easily recording everything that keeps coming to my mind:

- ♥ *Must have a great smile*
- ♥ *Must have good teeth (that's weird, but okay)*
- ♥ *Kind*
- ♥ *Patient*
- ♥ *Loving*
- ♥ *Must want a family*
- ♥ *Respects women and men as equals*
- ♥ *Loves dogs*
- ♥ *Hard worker*
- ♥ *Tall*
- ♥ *Confident*
- ♥ *Respectful*
- ♥ *Happy*
- ♥ *Can provide for his family*
- ♥ *Feels lucky to have me (that would feel nice)*
- ♥ *Wants to try new things*

I look at the list, reread it twice, and really start to think about what I've just written. It isn't anything profound, but everything I wrote is true to my heart. I didn't include anything outlandish like "must be good in bed" or "rich," just characteristics of a decent human being.

Mike jumps back in the car with one order of fries and Gatorade for himself. I look over at him and then back to my list. Something as simple as a little list suddenly makes everything clear; my heart plummets to my feet! To my horror, Mike only fits two of my criteria. This realization hits me hard, but as unsettling as this conclusion is, I don't feel panic arise. On the contrary, I feel like for the first time in a long time the fog has lifted, and I can see. My mind becomes clear; it is like I have 20/20 vision. I am transported back to Okanagan Lake, where when you are close to the shore and can see every detail of the rocks below. Every line, contour, and vibrant color through the crystal-clear water. That's how clear my mind is. Soon, that clarity is getting stockpiled with questions.

How is it possible he is none of these things? Did I make up who I thought he was? He is supposed to be my forever? Have I been living in a fantasy? If these criteria are what I value in a partner, then how can I be so committed to someone who holds none of these characteristics? It is this exact moment that I know Mike and I are not to be and that I deserve more. The promise of being with him forever had been a fantasy. My calm clarity begins twisting my stomach. I start breathing funny, trying to regulate my new awareness.

Mike looks over and tells me our line is moving as he stuffs a fry in his mouth.

I start the car and join the line. *Crap. This isn't who I should be with.* The clarity is nauseating, and we are on our way to his home to spend Christmas with his whole family. *Don't I need Mike?* I am petrified because I have also never had this kind of mental clarity. For the first time in nearly nine years, I know he and I are never going to happen. He is never going to be the man I want. And for the first time, I am thankful for how little attention he pays me. He isn't even looking over in my direction. If he had, he would have known I'm not okay. This confirms to me that his thoughts are usually only pointed at himself.

Sometimes it only takes a moment for your whole life to change, and that just happened to me. *Breathe. You will figure this out. Now go and put your smile on like you always do and enjoy Christmas.*

CHAPTER 2 – CELESTE

It was early April, and I was still living with Mike. My feelings hadn't changed since Christmas—I knew he wasn't the one—but I just didn't know how to leave. His health was the worst it had ever been, and I didn't know how to detangle our lives. I couldn't stay, but something was keeping me in the same pattern, the one where I looked after his needs and forgot how to look after my own.

I would go into work, then come home and find Mike on the couch with the same story as the day before. He was in pain and still hadn't done anything to make it better. He would wait for the next doctor's appointment, the doctor would refer him to another, then another. We made major changes to our diet and bought special food to help. This was a huge strain on my bank account because Mike wasn't working, and whenever he did spend money, it was always on himself.

So, I tried to make all the meals to help him feel better. While I read from the new vegan cookbook he got at Christmas, my mind wandered back to the holiday. I remember sitting there on Christmas morning as we passed out presents to one another. I got a beautiful piece of handmade art from his mother that was meaningful and gorgeous, and I knew it would be the last gift I would ever receive from her. I remember looking over at his dad, a man I truly cared for, and I was already feeling the loss of our relationship, knowing that his kind and thoughtful gestures would be coming to an end. And just like every other past holiday, Mike didn't propose, but for the first time, I was thankful.

I'd spent the months since then trying to figure out what my life would look like without Mike and his family. *How can I be brave enough to end what has been so comfortable? Who am I to ask for more or for what I really want?* I'd been settling year after year and accepting less and less . . . until now. I felt like I was trying to cross a raging river and couldn't see the other side. So, we returned after Christmas break and settled into our routine again, the only change being that I knew our relationship was over, and he didn't.

But my self-worth had become so low, and this feeling so normal, that I didn't have any idea how to break the habits we had built over the years. So, I kept making meals and feeling guilty that I wanted to leave someone who was off work on medical leave with me as their only support. This is what had become of our relationship; I was his caregiver. If I was going to leave, I needed him to be healthy, at least, so he could look after himself.

I woke up feeling hopeful. I had an interview for a new position at work and was visualizing the outcome: getting the job and the pay raise that goes with it. As I showered, I started preparing for the questions I'd be asked, reviewing my responses in my mind. I walked out of the bathroom with a towel wrapped around me so I could pick out my outfit. I needed to wear something super professional but not scream to my coworkers that I had an in-house interview. I picked my matching skirt and blazer with a white shirt and lay them on the bed.

I was back in the bathroom, adding mascara to my top lashes, when Mike came to the door, yelling that I was ignoring him.

I turned to look at him, confused. "I am listening, right now as I get—"

He leaned close to my face and yelled about a having a bad

dream. He wanted to tell me about it and was upset that I was more focused on getting ready for work, like I was some kind of hot shot and thought I was better than him.

There was no reasoning with him, so I quickly got dressed and left the apartment as fast as possible. I didn't want to give him any more time to start up again. I felt sick, but I needed to focus on my interview.

Him yelling that close to my face was almost an out-of-body experience. It was like I could see the interaction from above and knew I needed out. He should have been supporting me as I got ready for my big day, not telling me I had done something wrong again. He should know that we needed this raise now that he wasn't contributing to the finances. I wanted to cry but couldn't. It didn't matter what I did for him, it was never enough.

I don't think my self-esteem had ever felt so low, but the clarity I had back at Christmas returned. At least this time his words didn't penetrate. I knew I deserved better. Every other time these arguments happened, I always took responsibility for my actions—or inaction— and tried to make everything better. Him better. But now I knew I needed to get serious about finding a way to leave.

I walked to work along 10th Avenue. Being a few blocks up from Broadway meant it was a quiet stroll, stopping for every crossing light, which all seemed to be red that morning. My legs took me in the direction of work, but my mind was elsewhere so I wasn't able to enjoy the April blossoms on the trees or the sun peeking through the rain clouds. I was trying to prepare for the interview and find some inner confidence as my thoughts kept drifting back to the morning's yelling and an exit plan. Mike had never listened to my words or allowed space for me to stand up for myself. *So how the heck am I going to leave when I have never left before?* He had always left, and I had always stayed.

I gave myself a full body shake, bringing my mind back to the present. I had an interview to prepare for, so I put a smile on my face and walked in the main doors of the hospital. *One thing at a time, Celeste.*

A week later, we went to another medical appointment. For over a year, Mike's doctor had been referring him to specialists, who had no answers other than to refer us to another specialist. Apparently, going gluten-free wasn't making him much better, so we were meeting a gastroenterologist who was going to send Mike for more tests. I was really hoping this would bring him some answers because I knew this was a problem for him and not one I could fix.

After the appointment, I went back to the office and called Mike's grandma to give her an update. She had taught me so much about family and what it looked like to be a matriarch. She showed up time and time again for any family member, treating them with respect and honor, and helping in any way she could. I truly respected her, and her opinion had always mattered when it came to the relationships I had with Mike's family, the family I had grown to love as my own. Her gentle, caring nature had bonded us instantly. I know now that not being brave enough to leave her grandson had a lot to do with not disappointing her.

As we talked, she could hear in my voice how tired I was. Tired of looking after her grandson. She also knew it would never be enough, because no matter how much I looked after him, there was still no ring, and no commitment. While we were talking, she said, "Celeste, if you need to leave, we understand."

I just remember saying a soft "okay" in response and we didn't pursue it further, but we both knew exactly what she meant.

The moment she said it, I felt the weight of the world fall away. It was everything I needed to hear. It was the permission I had needed without realizing it. I now knew I would start my goodbyes to this family, to everything they had given me. I was allowed to look after myself, to leave a relationship that was no longer a relationship. She didn't elaborate, and she didn't need to.

I felt the shift within me, making me feel stronger. I could leave, even when he was weak. I could ask for what I wanted and deserved. I hung up and immediately started typing a letter to Mike. The words flowed out of me. I was not waiting any longer to end something that has carried on years longer than it should have. I printed the letter, put it in a blank envelope, and brought it home with me.

I walked into the apartment, took my shoes off, and sat across from him on the couch.

"Can you turn off the TV, please? I have something I need to talk to you about," I said calmly as I pet Lucy who sat between us.

He turned the TV down.

"I know this might come as a surprise, but really, it shouldn't. I have come to decision and have written it out in a letter. I want to read that letter to you."

He looked my way slightly, then turned back to the TV, watching the images.

I opened the letter and took a deep breath. "Dear Mike, I have arrived at a decision, and I need you to know that I didn't make this decision in haste. I have been thinking about you and me for a while now and it's become very clear that we no longer work well together, and I think we should break up. Our relationship has deteriorated over the years, and it feels like we are more just roommates these days. What we had was special and we have a lot of good memories together, but that just isn't enough for me. I also think by staying together, I am doing you a disservice. Your health and well-being are not getting better, and you don't seem to want to do anything to change that. I feel like I am the only one advocating for you. So, if we stay together, I am enabling your healing—"

He turned to face me on the couch but said nothing.

"So, I think it's time we end things. I will always love you and cherish our time together, and I know I will miss your family terribly. But I know this is the right decision for both of us. Love, Celeste."

I folded the letter back into the envelope and passed it to him. He took it.

It was such a relief to say this out loud, finally. Mike was a little shocked but didn't seem to think it was a big deal. But why would he? This was more of an inconvenience, if anything. He probably thought I'd change my mind, like every other time I took him back. He always left for his own needs, and I always accepted his reasons for returning. What he didn't know was that I was different this time, and I knew I would never be with him again. My heart was out.

He stared at the TV for a bit knowing I was staring at him, then said fine, he'd go live with his parents for a while to give me some time.

"Good idea, but I need you to know I'm not changing my mind. I don't need time. We are not getting back together."

He laughed and nodded his head sarcastically.

So, I left to get groceries. I needed some distance to collect myself. That almost felt too easy, but if he was willing to leave, that was all I wanted, so there was relief there. What was interesting is that I didn't feel any sadness. It felt long overdue. Maybe in time he would see that this was for the best.

He packed a small bag and left in the morning, almost like it was normal and nothing had changed. But everything had changed for me. I knew there was no going back for us. I appreciated him giving me time without him in the apartment, because I needed to get my bearings, gather some strength, and start looking after myself. I didn't even know what "me first" looked like.

In the weeks after he left, I began a list and made arrangements for what parts of our lives needed to be untangled, starting with slowly gathering his belongings and placing them in boxes. One large obstacle was his sister's upcoming wedding in two months in which I was a bridesmaid. I called her a week after Mike left and said I didn't think it would be a good idea for me to still be in her wedding, but she didn't believe me when I said we would not be getting back together this time. So, she asked me to stay in the wedding party because she cared about me, even if I wasn't together with Mike. I mean, I did understand her sentiment: we had known each other for years and had become friends and had made a lot of memories together. Therefore, I believed her when she said she still wanted me to be a bridesmaid and that we could still be friends.

It was now July, and I still hadn't seen Mike since he left. He texted a few times asking about our cat, Lucy, but I never gave much of a response and kept it short. I made it clear that I still didn't want to get back together and as much as I hoped he believed me, I think he was just giving me space until I changed my mind, got lonely, and begged him to come back. So, he carried on doing his own thing, either at his parents' place or his grandparents' apartment.

After being on my own for a few months, I started feeling lighter and more at ease. It was like I could finally relax, finally breathe deeply on my own. Everything was easier without him. I didn't want Mike back and never would. I was feeling stronger every day, more confident in myself, and I wanted to keep this trend going.

We had our last bridesmaid dress fitting late July, and I tried again to tell his sister that I shouldn't be in the wedding party. But she still wanted me there. In retrospect, knowing how I felt, I should have declined and walked away, but at that time in my life, I'd always done what people asked of me, starting at age eleven.

My first ten years of life were as perfect as they could be. My brother and I had two parents devoted to our family, giving us space for whoever we were as kids and loving every little piece of us. We could do no wrong and felt nothing but love every day from both Mom and Dad. Our dad used to wake us up while it was still dark out so we could catch the fresh powder up at the local ski hill. He coached both our soccer teams and took us golfing in the blaze of the summer sun. My mom looked after our health and well-being. I knew I hit the jackpot when it came to my parents. I was adored, and I loved them fiercely.

But everything changed when I turned eleven and my parents divorced. It was sudden and not amicable. My cherished father, who had made me his number one girl, found a new woman and made her his number one. So, I went from having the undivided, trustworthy love from a parent to losing it overnight, which made me try really hard to do whatever it would take to get his attention back. As a result, I learned new emotional habits including splitting myself into smaller pieces so perhaps some would be accepted, molding myself into versions that just might please or be "enough," and anticipating others' needs first to make sure not to provoke so I could stay. But it seemed that the more I tried, the more I lost my dad, and it skewed my equilibrium for setting boundaries and having a sense of self-worth.

So, it was no surprise that when I was pushed to be part of the wedding, I relented. I didn't want to make anyone else unhappy. I should have stayed away from the event altogether, but my weak boundaries won out, and I was at the wedding. Mike kept looking at me during the ceremony, and when we were all posing for photos on the beach with the Pacific Ocean in the background, I remained distant but civil. Fortunately, one of the other bridesmaids offered me a bed at her parents' place and even allowed Lucy to stay. I think she was the only one who believed me when I said we were done, and I truly appreciated her respecting my needs.

Throughout the day of the wedding, I took moments to talk with different family members I had bonded with over the years, secretly trying to convey to them how they had made an impact on my life. I had a minute alone with Mike's grandma during the reception when we sat together at one of the tables after dinner.

"Celeste, you look absolutely beautiful today," she said, then brought me in for a big hug.

I pulled her into me tightly, holding her longer than I usually would. When I broke away, I looked her straight in the eyes. "I love you, and I always will."

"And I love you too, Celeste."

"I want you to know that your kindness over the years impacted me. I watched how you look after your family, and it's very admirable. I hope one day to lead my family the same way you do yours."

She brought me in for another hug and whispered in my ear, "And I have no doubt that you will, and whoever gets to love you will be one lucky man."

A knowing look passed between us. A goodbye. Our eyes glistened with unshed tears and respect until the moment was broken by her son-in-law, another man I adored, asking her to dance.

When I left the brunch the morning after, I said a final goodbye to some I truly loved, to their homes, and to their town, then drove to the ferry with Lucy and cried. I cried for what was and what could have been and for the relief I felt now that it was over. I had never felt so insecure and yet so confident in a decision my whole life. Somewhere deep in my heart I knew this was right. I was going to be okay.

CHAPTER 3 – CELESTE

I returned to the apartment, thankful I was the one keeping it. After all, I had found this place, so Mike knew he couldn't ask me to leave. Even though I had already had a few months on my own without him, now that the wedding was over, it felt final. The only parts left of Mike were his things along the back wall that he would need to pick up.

I felt ready for the next chapter of my life. It was open, blank, and ready for me to fill it in with whatever I wanted. I started by eating as much gluten as possible. I ate fast food like it was going out of style, plus a lot of mac and cheese.

On some days I felt low and scared, so I'd smoke a J and cuddle with my cat. Mike and I had gotten Lucy about a year prior from his aunt who couldn't keep her. She had been the best part of my days and always lightened my mood. She loved to "talk." Every morning when I was in the shower, she'd come in and meow the entire time. And when I'd get out, she'd lick my legs. I was so thankful to have her company while I navigated the end of my era with Mike. She would wait for me for when I got home, and always gave me a warmer welcome than Mike ever had. She helped me forget I was starting over and how vulnerable I felt. I was thirty-one years old and on a timeline if I ever wanted to start a family. And if my relationship with Mike had taught me anything, it was that it could take a long time to get to a proposal, not to mention having kids. I cried and grieved and allowed myself a lot of self-pity, all the while flirting with the notion that just maybe I had opened myself up to possibilities that I could find someone who deserved me. And maybe I would know my own worth by then too.

Each day, I felt a little stronger and a little braver. *Who was I before Mike?* It felt like such a big question. I really had no idea. I knew I was nice and thoughtful of others, but what did I like? So, I made a commitment to try new things and get myself out in the world.

It was time to start living again, and who better to help than my closest girlfriend, Dallas, so I called her. "What are you up to?"

"Nothing."

"Want to go to the beach?"

"Ready in thirty minutes."

Dallas had supported me through some of the crap with Mike, but she wasn't around for all of it, and I had kept some things from her. She didn't know how low I felt, but she was the best at making me feel better.

I got ready for a day at the beach with some hope in my chest. It had been a hot minute since I'd interacted with the opposite sex, and it felt liberating to be single. I was really excited and a little terrified. I put my cutest sundress on top of my bathing suit and packed some water, a towel, and my favorite companion, *InStyle*—a magazine so full of color it always brightened my mood even if it felt like an indulgence. Dallas drove to my place from the house she lived in with her husband in North Vancouver so we could walk together.

I lived in a fairly run-down apartment building in Kitsilano. However, no matter how run-down it was, it was mine and I could afford it and it allowed me to live in one of the most beautiful places in the world. This particular place is even better when you're single. Kits (as the locals call it) has everything one needs within twelve blocks, with a beautiful beach on the edge of the Pacific Ocean at the bottom of a hill. Not only is it picturesque, it has a special feeling. It's so beautiful, it's like you know you're part of a cool gang just by being there.

Dallas and I found a small open patch of grass among the other nearby beachgoers, set out our towels, and looked out across the inlet to the other side where there were also multiple beaches on the edge of Stanley Park.

We started our day by checking out all the guys around us, as that had been our favorite pastime since our teenage years. Boys, boys, boys. We watched a group of boys (men) throw a football around. They were completely chiseled with some muscles a little too large in places for me. I was probably being critical because it made me self-conscious of my little belly and reminded me that I really should go to the gym. Buff guys can be attractive, but it might mean they perhaps aren't interested in having a spouse who isn't as fit, which had certainly never been a priority for me. I purposely thought *spouse* because I was not looking to date. I was thirty-one years old and wasn't interested in something casual.

I was lost in thought, then brought back to reality when a football hit our towel. I grabbed it and threw it back with a big dumb smile on my face. *Argh, why do I have to feel desperate?* It was becoming very obvious to me how low my self-worth had become, as I was now questioning every interaction I had with the opposite sex. I groaned out loud.

"What should we do tonight?" I asked Dallas.

She grinned. She had always been a great sport and knew me so well. "Well, we now have a bit of a glow from the sun, so let's head somewhere for a drink, maybe some dancing."

I smiled and nodded eagerly.

"I'll text around and see what's going on."

"Love it! I am going to get a little more glow on," I said, settling back onto my towel, feeling ready for adventure.

"How are you really doing these days?" Dallas raised her sunglasses and turned toward me on her blanket.

I peeked up at her from under my shades. "I think I'm doing okay, just ready to move on, you know?"

"Yeah, I get it, but remember you were with Mike for a long time. It's okay to not really know how to feel these days. Your focus was on him for so long."

"Yeah, that's where I'm at right now. Pissed at myself. Like now that I can see our relationship clearly, I don't know how I stayed so long! It's like I had to make sure I stayed with him until I had nothing left in the tank . . . like how low could I really feel?"

"Well, we don't always know it when we are in it. It was hard to watch you fawn over him over the years, knowing he never deserved you, but we were also young and in our twenties, and you can't always see things clearly."

"Okay, fair. But remember who I was in high school?"

"Oh yeah! I remember how many of the boys followed you around like the queen you were."

I laughed. "That girl! Yeah, I remember her too. I didn't really care about boys. I mean, I was boy crazy, but I never *cared* to really be with them. And the ones I had huge crushes on usually had me wimping out and just watching them from afar."

"So which one are you thinking of now? Josh or Travis?"

"Okay, no one can match the crush I had on Josh. I couldn't believe it when I got to make out with him too."

"Three times if I remember correctly, including at my parents' Christmas party." She laughed at the memory.

"OMG, and your mom interrupted us. 'Celeste, you better not be in there with a boy!' Oh, I was mortified." It felt good to remember happier times. It had been so easy for us in high school.

"He wanted to go out with you that summer."

"I remember, but I chickened out. For some reason, the boys I really liked had me shying away. It's like I would forget how to act normal. If only I'd had the guts to keep talking with Josh. He made it clear he was interested, and I was crushing hard. Well, I am ready to get back to the girl who was confident and didn't *need* to have a man."

"Good, I am ready to have my old friend back. She sure did enjoy life." She gave me a last look before checking her phone. "Sweet! Sam is in town with some friends from her program and they are heading to the Roxy tonight. Shall we?"

"Yes! it's been years since I've seen Sam. Perfect timing." Sam was another good friend from high school who I'd lost touch with over the course of my relationship with Mike. It would be great to see her.

We packed up our bags and started the hike up the hill. At the end of ten blocks straight up, we were huffing and puffing. Back at my place, we mixed some drinks, put on some Mary J. Blige, and decided to wear something sexy for our evening out.

As exciting as it felt to have plans on a warm Saturday in Vancouver, I knew I had no money. I thought I might have enough for the cover charge and maybe one drink once we were inside. Getting a cab was a luxury, so we'd walk, if we had to.

As I flicked through the hangers in my closet, I had no idea what to wear. Everything looked cheap to me, probably because I could only afford things from the sales rack, so I didn't have anything I really loved.

"I don't know what to wear!" I yelled from my bedroom.

"Well, nothing new there. How many years did I dress you?"

"Yes, you did. You and your mom taught me everything I know. But look at what I have. None of it looks good."

She rummaged through my options and pulled out a beige tank. "What about this one? It looks tight and sexy and it's time you dressed like the beauty you are."

I rolled my eyes. "I do like this one; it hides the muffin top."

"Oh, shut it, you don't have a muffin top. You've always been tall and slender with zero cellulite. Now it's time to own that body." She handed me the top and walked into the bathroom to finish her makeup.

"Easy for you to say, you always had a booty and boobs to show off your hourglass figure."

"I'm not playing the 'poor me' game, Celeste. You're a stunner and always have been."

I put on the tank and my tightest jeans, then curled my hair and added a little more makeup than usual. I looked in the mirror and liked what I saw. I wondered what it would feel like to look in the mirror and actually love the person looking back. I gave myself a small smile and grabbed my purse and Dallas on my way out the door.

We felt a little tipsy as we headed downtown to meet our friends at the Roxy. Dallas paid for a cab, God bless her, as I didn't know how I would have made it to Granville Street in my heels. We spotted Sam and her friends in line and made our way over, passing a busker on the street corner and a few trendy restaurants on the way. Most of us had just gotten cell phones for the first time and were mostly just using them for texting. There were no selfies yet because the quality was so grainy. We were just a bunch of '80's kids out at night in the city and feeling free as birds, living in over-priced apartments but independent. I breathed in the city air and felt great.

"I always forget the vibe of Granville Street at night; it's like everyone comes out."

"It's been a while since I have been downtown, if I am being honest. Thanks for getting me out."

Sam enveloped me in a huge hug as soon as we joined her, and it felt like another piece of home. We linked arms and ignored the glares behind us like we didn't just cut in line.

Dallas and I danced until our feet hurt, and I didn't even care that I couldn't afford drinks. Our favorite beats reminded us of simpler times. I had planned to check out the men, but instead, I spent the night on the dance floor, which is just what I needed. It felt good to just let loose and move to the music. To not think about who I was or who I wasn't.

CHAPTER 4 – CELESTE

Things were getting easier every day as I figured out my routine without Mike. I had compromised a lot of who I was when I was with him and now was the time to rediscover myself, so I started saying yes to as many things as possible. When a friend asked me to join the beach volleyball league, I agreed, even though I hadn't played since high school. I felt like I couldn't not play beach volleyball considering I lived within walking distance of the ocean with beaches everywhere.

The team, which met every Wednesday evening, was mostly made up of law students and was a rec league, just for fun. I didn't know anyone on the team except my friend Joel before joining. He had mostly gathered the team through those from his law classes and his new firm. There were seven of us on the team, which meant we only had one sub. Playing in the sand was harder than I had imagined, but everyone was so easygoing, considering they were either in law school or articling, which I had come to understand was a competitive and stressful career path. There were two women and the rest men, all in our thirties and single. One man was particularly cute, and we seemed to hit it off right away, with easy banter back and forth. And he was always encouraging me, whether I actually connected a spike over the net or landed flat on my face while diving for the ball. He gave me genuine smiles, and I liked the feeling of his eyes finding mine. We usually just showed up, played the three games, then went home, but after a few weeks, we started hanging back after the others had left and chatting on the slow walk to our cars. He seemed so kind and down to earth, but he didn't ask me out.

Eight weeks later, after our final game, the team decided to go out for drinks afterward. In the break between our games, Gabriel approached me. It felt like this was my opportunity to see if what I was feeling was mutual.

As he walked up with a big smile, I blurted out, "Would you like to get a drink sometime, just you and me?" I couldn't believe that it came out of my mouth. I'd never asked a guy out before and was trying to get my confidence back.

He grinned, and after what felt like forever, he finally responded: "I would like that, but I should say it would just be as friends."

I looked at the ground. "Oh, okay, well, I wasn't looking for another friend."

"I'm honored you asked, but I should have been clear that I do have a girlfriend."

I blinked a few times because this was the first I'd heard of him seeing anyone. "Thank you for being honest, but it's probably best we don't get that drink then," I said quickly before walking away.

We played our last game and I tried to avoid his eyes the whole time. I felt so embarrassed, but we still had that team drink to go to. Great.

The pub was a few blocks away from the courts and we all drove there separately. I made sure everyone sat down first so that I could sit furthest away from Gabriel. I was able to chat with those at my end of the table. I really felt like disappearing, but whenever I glanced his way, Gabriel didn't look fazed in the least. I had one drink, then made my way around the table saying my goodbyes and thanking everyone for a fun time. I couldn't bolt fast enough. Joel didn't think anything of it, and Gabriel gave me a very platonic hug goodbye.

When I got in my car, I texted Dallas. This was my first time asking someone out, and I felt mortified.

Me: Guess what I did?

> Dallas: Stripped naked and ran through the volleyball courts

Me: Worse

> Dallas: It can't be worse than all our friends knowing the moment you lost your virginity

Me: Argh! Don't remind me. Okay, you know that guy I was telling you about from volleyball?

> Dallas: Yeah

Me: Well, I asked him out

> Dallas: Nice! When are you guys going out?

Me: He shot me down because he has a girlfriend and then I had to sit at the bar having a drink with the team afterward acting like I didn't just expose myself

> Dallas: Get over it! His loss. And get over the dramatics. It's 2009! You're not the first woman to ask a guy out

Me: Then why do I feel so low and scared?

> Dallas: Because you put yourself out there and your confidence is at an all-time low, so it stung. But don't let how Mike treated you to stay with you. You're a catch and it's time you remembered that

Me: Thank you. I needed that : -

Dallas: I know who you are and you have never needed a man. So, if this guy isn't your man, at least you didn't waste any more time wondering. I am proud of you. Now get him out of your head, put your shoulders back, and hold your head high. You're fucking Celeste, and any man would be lucky to have you

Me: You're the best. I love you. Going to drive home now before it rains any harder

As I drove home, I wondered why I felt so dejected. The old me would have laughed it off or never even cared in the first place. If I am being honest, I think it's because I could have sworn Gabriel was interested and now it just made me think it had been all in my head. Was my active imagination playing tricks on me? If so, it made me feel like I couldn't trust myself. I didn't like that Mike was still in my head, making me doubt myself and my actions.

I took a big breath and thought about the night. Dallas was right. Look at how brave I was: maybe I *should* be proud of myself for asking him out. I mean, I hiked the West Coast Trail topless for heaven's sake. I used to have so much confidence; I'd been bold and not worried about what anyone else thought of me. Maybe I wasn't as far off as I thought from the former Celeste.

I had always lived in a fantasy land when it came to my dreams for the future, forever the hopeless romantic when it came to life. But I liked that part of me, always trying new things and believing in possibilities. So, my dream of having a family, a home on a quiet street, maybe even two boys and a husband who adored me, well, I decided to keep that one alive in my thoughts.

I remember arriving in Vancouver so confident and full of optimism. There was nothing I didn't want to try, and the city felt like the catalyst to living even larger. Having so many possibilities felt so exciting. I thought about trying some acting classes or joining a ski club. My outlook was as sunny and bright as my outfits—nothing gray or black for miles.

The first week in Vancouver sailed by, and I was so excited to go out with some friends from high school that first weekend. I was saying yes to most things and even had my first hookup with my friend's roommate. It was Mike.

I remember waking up the next morning and feeling confused and a little desperate, feelings I wasn't familiar with. And then slowly, my days started feeling colorless. Maybe Mike put a spell on me because I craved his attention after that first night. My guy friend, his roommate, tried to warn me about him. He saw my changing behavior and tried to ring the alarm bells that I wasn't acting like myself, but I was determined to be with Mike. Then, over the years, I gradually seemed to lose myself and forget what I wanted.

Finally, now nine years later, I was starting over in Vancouver. On my own. Maybe I could find that girl who moved to the city so full of hope, the one who didn't shy away from anything and went after what she wanted, knowing anything was possible and living like life was to be lived with the volume cranked high and loud.

Even though I was dead broke, I loved living in Vancouver, and it offered so much in return. My apartment was sparse, made up of hand-me-down kitchen supplies, second-hand IKEA furniture with a new wicker bed, which I loved, and a new comfortable couch I had splurged on. All of it was neatly arranged in a fifty-year-old building, which had never been updated, but my apartment was the top floor, in the corner, with a separate bedroom. I felt like I had hit the jackpot because it was all mine.

I didn't have internet or extra spending money, but I was independent and looking after myself, and that felt good. And I had a really great job that I walked to every day. I'd worked there for five years, and my colleagues felt like family. I was one of the younger ones on staff, so all the senior staff looked out for me. I had great connections and friendships and felt lucky to finally be living the life I had meant to live when I moved to Vancouver all those years ago. My decisions were mine, and the consequences were mine too.

Summer faded and fall arrived. I finally arranged for Mike to collect his things and leave his key. He said he would come while I was at work. I didn't hear from him all day, so I nervously opened the door that evening. It was quiet. I looked at the corner at the back of the living room and all his things were gone. He'd come and gone.

I sat on the couch, closed my eyes, and took a deep breath. I felt the weight of him in my life slowly leaving my shoulders. I don't know how long I was there until I realized it was really quiet. Too quiet. Lucy usually would have jumped on the couch by then, talking to me, welcoming me home. I called for her. Nothing. I walked around and looked in the cupboards and under my bed. Then I realized her kitty litter was gone. *He didn't!*

I called Mike. He answered immediately.

"You took Lucy?"

"Yes, I did. Why do you care?"

"How could you? She has been living with me, and I have been looking after her," I said through sobs.

"How could I? You're the one being a bitch here. Do you know how hard that was for me to see all my stuff packed up?"

"Yeah. Mike, we broke up, and I didn't want your stuff here anymore."

"We didn't break up, Celeste. We were on a break, and if you are crying, you obviously know you made a mistake."

"I did not make a mistake. We are done and have been for a long time. Stop acting like a victim here. You know we haven't worked for years."

"I didn't agree to this, and you have been acting like a selfish child. I just went along with it because I thought you would realize you made a mistake."

His seething was actually making me feel calmer about the situation. "It's not a mistake. We are over."

"Well, when you get your head out of your ass and realize that you need me, let me know, then you can see Lucy again!" he shouted before hanging up.

I put my phone down and stared at the wall. He also hadn't returned the key.

Nothing had ever been honest with him. He'd always made me doubt myself, but this time, I could hear how condescending he was because I had distance from him. I was able to be objective and see how taking Lucy was another way of him trying to control me. Now I understood why he hadn't bothered me much at the wedding; he had been waiting for me to change my mind like I had in the past. But I wasn't that person anymore. When I wrote that list in the car that day at the ferry terminal, something changed in me. It made me believe that I could have more. Maybe even have the life I deserve.

That night I had a pity party. I was angry and sad over how much longer our relationship had been than it needed to be until I finally let go of the hope I'd held on to for all those years when I thought he was my soulmate. The blunt truth is that he never was. I only saw what I wanted to, and my insecurity in myself made me stay way longer than I should have. Over and over he showed me who he was, and I always excused his behavior. He was an angry, bitter man who took my cat out of spite. *Crap, if he is just processing this now, what might he do?*

The next day, on my lunch break, I bought a lock with a deadbolt. *Hopefully, he won't go back to the apartment before I get home from work.* Mike had shown me over and over that he couldn't be trusted, but now I finally believed him. I took a deep breath and thought of the list and my future. *You can do this, Celeste,* I kept repeating to myself.

I walked home quickly and held my breath as I looked around the apartment to see if he'd come back. Everything looked just like I'd left it that morning. I grabbed my screwdriver and carefully followed the instructions to replace the lock with a new deadbolt. I felt so proud of myself as I tested the new key. It worked. I really did it. I felt empowered, which was an emotion I hadn't felt often in my life. And I felt safe and secure, knowing that if he came now, he wouldn't be able to get in. *I have finally chosen myself. I've chosen boundaries.* Something shifted in me when I changed that lock. Maybe something was shifting in my universe too.

I slept really well that night.

It was a typical rainy Tuesday in October. I was at work, and I walked down the stairs from my office to the main floor where the mail was kept behind the reception desk. Out of the corner of my eye I saw the profile of a tall, dark-haired man sitting in a chair in the adjacent office.

I turned to see more. He was wearing bike shorts and a tight-fitting black-and-red top. *That's an odd outfit to be wearing for a meeting.* He was in the office of the new AVP of Operations, who, I remembered, had posted for a research officer position.

This man had great posture, he appeared to be fit (at least if his bicycle gear was anything to go by), and he was signing some paperwork. I stared as casually as possible while taking longer than usual to grab the mail, trying to crane my neck to see his face. I don't know if it was the profile or the dark curly hair, but a thought passed through me—a single fleeting thought that barely even registered; a whisper: *There he is.*

I grabbed the mail, went to the bathroom to compose myself, then walked back to the main reception doors just in case I could get one more glimpse of this mysterious man.

CHAPTER 5 – DAVE

Of course it's raining. I just hope my new boss doesn't decide to introduce me to everyone in the office with a streak of brown water up my back. I've got to get my license and a car. This constant cycling is getting tiresome. To be honest, the ride to the Hospital Foundation is pretty direct from home, so the commute will be doable. And I do love cycling along 10th Avenue, especially this time of year. The leaves are changing and it's not too cold yet, though cold enough. I love having the ocean in view with the city sitting in the foreground.

I moved to Vancouver four years ago from Toronto, and it feels so fresh and clean by comparison. I never really liked Toronto. Too much go-go-go, too many cars, and too many people. Here, it can be busy, but you're always so close to nature, you can kind of tune it out if you want to. My parents had moved out here about ten years ago and settled on Vancouver Island. I visited for Christmas one year and there was no snow. After Ontario winters, that was enough for me. It was a no-brainer to move here. I tried the island first but couldn't swing it. Loved how it felt, though. The longer I was in BC, the more I wanted to stay.

My favorite thing in Vancouver is walking Tibby in the Endowment Lands and Spanish Banks. Always endless invigorating trails to explore. I feel at peace. Good thing, because my personal life has been dismal. Still, I'm glad Deirdre went back to Toronto. That was seven years of my life I'm not getting back. Seven years—it hurts to think about it. Seems like such a waste. Deirdre always just took and took and gave nothing back in return, and I let that happen. No one to blame but myself. I don't know what happened, maybe the trigger of being in my mid-thirties with no family, of watching her enroll in degree after degree, a permanent student, permanently unemployed. Finally, I snapped: "You have to get a job." And with that, she departed. No argument, no blowup, simply a departure. I didn't even care that she left. I actually felt better. You couldn't pull the constant smile off my face. It was like a whole new world opened up for me, but I didn't even know where I wanted to go or what I wanted to do. It was a summer of discovery. I watched movies that I actually liked. I watched sports. I got season tickets to the Whitecaps. It turns out I'd rather go to a pub than a coffee shop, and I have no interest in attending gallery openings. Who knew? *Why didn't I do that six years ago when I knew she wasn't the one? How did I lose myself in a relationship so utterly and completely?* I still can't answer those questions. It was such a slow, aimless grind to the bottom that I can't retrace my steps.

Dating these past few years has been about as much fun as a colonoscopy. Looking for love in a bar rarely works out, so I tried online dating because that's how a friend met her future husband. But man, what a trip! Lots of lunch dates and coffees, which suits me fine, except for the company. I bet I've "dated" about twenty-five people in total, with about fifteen in person. I didn't make it past the phone interview in a few cases. I was pretty straightforward in my bio: "Must Love Dogs," which is both a truth and a tip of the hat that I also enjoy a good rom-com. I tried to cover all the bases within the defined character allowance, but you only really know when you meet face-to-face. Sometimes I knew it was a no-go before I sat down, others became obvious during the course of an Americano. Most had no interest in me whatsoever. I could tell because they never asked any questions. They simply enjoyed talking about themselves and seemed oblivious that I had given up my attention after about five sips and proceeded to look out the window.

Mid-thirties can be a challenge. You're reviewing your life choices and, if you're dating, attempting a course correction. What that course correction is can vary. Some realize they have been hyper-focused on their careers and achievements, wanting you to have the same interest in them so you can chart that course together. But I don't have any strong interest in my career. Don't get me wrong, I take my job seriously and I'm good at it, but my work philosophy is simple: I am being paid to do a job, so I do it. My second, more general, philosophy is that whatever you do in life, do the very best you can. So, I do well at my job, but to say I enjoy it would be an overstatement.

Women realize that the window for starting a family is narrow, much like myself, and they are also attempting a course correction. Backgrounds vary greatly here. Some are recently divorced or ending long-term relationships, all are in some degree of trauma and I totally get that, but how you handle that trauma while dating is the key. Maybe I had a juvenile expectation of dating, but I didn't think it would be so transactional. I thought that when we weren't together, we would at least be thinking about each other, longing for each other is a bit of a stretch, but I expected at least a general excitement about the whole thing. But it was a strange process. If I dated someone and didn't hear back, I picked up the message quickly and moved on, but there were times when I would be on a third or fourth date but would not hear from them in between each date: no text, no phone call, and then they would call me or even stop by the apartment unannounced and then vanish again. From my perspective, I was constantly thinking about the other person. What I liked about her, her smell, her voice, and I couldn't wait to see her. I would call but not hear back in days, or even weeks. This was the very beginning of a relationship; shouldn't we be madly excited? I didn't know what to make of it, so I decided that if it wasn't what I wanted, then I would walk. Mostly, I would politely decline a second date and they would look at me, perplexed. Then, the old thoughts of "just try harder" would creep in again.

Finally, I met someone the old-fashioned way. I met Jenn at the dog beach, which checked the dog box instantly. And I liked her dog, Wally, so bonus. But no matter how much you try, you can't base a relationship on the dogs, and it quickly fell apart. I tried to do whatever it was that she wanted from me, but I was not being myself, and if you can't be yourself, then the relationship is doomed. I vowed I wasn't going to make the same mistake I had with Deirdre and "stick it out" with her, but I did. I knew well before it got this bad that it was over, but after all the dismal dates before meeting her, I told myself that I was the problem and I had to make the changes. It made sense at the time. After all, the only constant variable in this dating equation was me, so what other conclusion could I make? We made plans, I even brought up children and she said "eventually." Good enough for me! Let's buy a townhouse!

What the hell was I thinking? She constantly criticized me. She didn't like my cooking and gave me a glare every time I had a beer even though she chugged a bottle of red every night. She didn't like the way I folded laundry or the way I loaded the dishwasher. One time, I brought her a coffee from the local coffee shop instead of Starbucks and she lost it. Everything was hard. So, I just needed to try harder. Six months later and I have no more trying left. Now, I live at the gym, work late, eat out, and sleep on the sofa. All my thoughts are focused on my new life. I've given up on a family at this point. I'm thirty-seven and tired of dating. It won't be a bad life, just a different life. A life with Tibby, but on my own. We will travel down the coast, see the island and the interior, go for long walks, find friends, and have fun. *It'll be okay.*

So, here I am, signing the paperwork for my new job. I sit across from my new boss, who seems like he understands me so far. I am pessimistic by nature, but I have a sense that this job might be the start of something new. I get up from my chair, shake hands with him, and head out of the office, but not before being distracted by rainbow tights. *That's an interesting choice.* I scan up the tights to a slender body on the way to a small smile that knocks the wind out of me temporarily. I catch my breath and shake my head and leave through the main doors of the hospital toward my bike, completely unsure if it was those tights or the smile that caught me off balance.

I bike home, feeling better than I have in a while. New job, feeling clear on ending things with Jenn, and ready for what is ahead.

CHAPTER 6 – CELESTE

Last year, I joined a floor hockey team. It gave me something of my own to do that got me out of the house while Mike was there. There is something empowering about playing in a sport that is all made up of women. The whole league was women of all different shapes, sizes, and ages. Novice or experienced, everyone just had a blast. I loved the drive, the determination, the encouragement, and the comradery. After every game, which most times we lost, I felt liberated and confident. I am so thankful I was welcomed on this team, where I was still learning but trying my damnedest to get a goal, which did happen once.

Floor hockey also brought in another blessing after I ended my relationship with Mike. Someone on the team was looking to rehome their cat, and I immediately offered. I had been missing Lucy's company so much. His name was Max, and he's a male brown tabby, much larger than Lucy. He didn't talk like Lucy did but loved to cuddle on the couch. Things were starting to turn around.

I spent most of my time on my own now that I wasn't in a relationship, and I learned to enjoy my own company. Playing floor hockey and soccer helped fill the social need. I didn't feel scared inside anymore, but hopeful.

To wet my toes in the dating world, I thought I should try online dating. Dallas had met her husband that way, so maybe that was the way to proceed. I also realized there wasn't any rush here. I had been spending almost all my time between my girlfriends, work, and sports, and I was starting to remember who I was and what I liked. Thinking back, I couldn't remember ever being on a first date, so this time of life felt exciting.

I started with a free version, but that seemed to attract a certain quality of men. I began connecting with a few men and having conversations, but I only said yes to meeting one of them in person. And this first interaction was enough for me to get a taste of how awkward online dating can be. The man I agreed to meet for coffee looked tall, dark, and handsome in his yoga poses on his profile. But when I saw him walking toward me, he just seemed to get smaller and shorter until I finally realized it wasn't an illusion. He was almost a foot shorter than me. Then, when the conversation stalled, I found a reason to leave.

I remember for certain that one of the items on my list for an ideal mate is being tall, and I wasn't about to settle. I knew what I deserved, and I didn't think I was asking for anything outlandish; being tall myself, I knew I wanted to be with someone equal to or taller than I am. When I first hit my growth spurt, it was before the boys in high school, so I habitually hunched over so I didn't make others feel less than. But now, as I have grown into the woman I am, I am proud of my height and want to walk with my shoulders back and head held high.

After that disappointing date, I needed to step up my game if I wanted something more serious, so I went to the paid platforms. I used money I didn't have and signed up for eHarmony: the biggest rage in online dating with commercials on every TV station to prove it.

I quickly realized why people pay for dating sites. It looked like people were taking this seriously. These were men with actual jobs. It gave me focus. I could filter through who wanted to talk with me and who I might want to exchange in conversation with. I talked with the first match. We had a lot in common, so we chatted back and forth for a few weeks until deciding to meet up for a drink.

We met at a local pub on a rainy Wednesday evening. Our conversations had been effortless and interesting on the online chats, so my imagination went into overdrive that he could be "the guy," and I was all nerves.

The date didn't end up going anywhere as there was no spark, but he was kind, and it was nice to try out a decent first date and survive. This whole dating world was starting to feel real. It felt good to see what could be possible.

The next day while eating my lunch at my desk so I could check out profiles, I closed my browser and looked up to see a passing figure. It was him, the new guy I had seen on that random Tuesday. I remember seeing the general email announcement come through, so I knew he had started earlier that week and yet I hadn't seen him until now. The announcement hadn't provided details about who he was, just that he had been working at various research positions for nonprofits across Canada and they had high hopes for him. Name: Dave Pennington. Sounded like a dream to me.

To be honest, I had been waiting for the official introduction. Usually, when a new staff member is hired, they are walked around and introduced to all the other staff members, but for some reason, that hadn't happened with Dave. So, I had the incentive to eat lunch at my desk, just in case it was time for introductions.

Of course, Dave was in Operations. Why couldn't he have been in Communications or Events where people are more social and we might have ended up in the same meetings? I felt like I was being left to my own devices to figure out how to meet him. And now, as I watched him walk right in front of me, my mouth hung open. He walked so confidently, like he really had somewhere to go.

I recalled the day I saw him leaving the office when I was returning. His head was down and then slowly he raised his eyes to meet mine, and it was like time stood still; it felt cosmic. My lady parts were on high alert just from this short encounter. He did look a little startled, but that's probably because he hadn't expected to see anyone coming through the door.

That afternoon we were having a staff meeting. I was hopeful it might mean introductions would be made. I arrived at the last minute. Thankfully, my good friend Sophie saved me a seat and I slid in. Sophie always had my back. It didn't matter how wild my antics got, she was always there for it. She found it hilarious watching me trying to date in the Vancouver scene, because she was single too. She knew the pain of it but decided to not make it any more difficult than it needed to be so didn't date at all. But she supported me.

The boardroom housed up to forty people comfortably. When someone walked into the room, they were immediately welcomed by a wall of windows that showcased the North Shore Mountains. My favorite thing in the room was the vibrant oil painting that covered the whole far wall space and had every color of the sun on it, all mixed together in harmony. Most meetings in this room had me dreaming of owning this painting one day, because looking at it made me feel like it knew me. However, something else drew my attention away from the splatter of color on this day.

The CEO walked in to start the meeting and first on the agenda was New Staff. There was a new person in Events who introduced herself as Ann, then, when prompted, shared something unique people might not know about her and a hobby. Suddenly things got interesting: it was time for the bike guy to speak. He stood tall, over six feet. He had dark eyes, but I couldn't tell the exact color from where I was sitting, and a mop of curly short brown hair.

If I could spell out my type, there he stood. Except for the navy cardigan—interesting choice.

"Hi, everyone, I'm Dave. Happy to be here in the Research Department." So far, so good; clear and confident. "I believe that being a librarian will help me with this job. Something personal about me, well, people like to call me Betty Crocker because I like to bake." This got a little chuckle from around the room. Dave sat down, and if I'm being honest, his introduction left me a little confused.

The rest of the meeting went by in a blur because I wasn't invested in the discussion unless it directly affected my bosses. I supported three directors. It was the new job I was interviewing for the morning Mike had yelled at me, and despite how rattled I had been, I pulled off an epic interview and had gotten the promotion.

The meeting finished and Sophie and I shuffled back to our desks. She had a grin on her face, and we were both thinking the same thing. I shut the two of us in her office and laughed out loud as she started to chuckle too.

I started. "Wears cardigans, is a librarian, and confidently shares he likes to bake." I snorted.

Sophie grinned. "I was thinking the same thing. Do you think he is straight?"

"Well, that changes everything."

"Sorry, did I miss something? What is this changing exactly?"

"Well, if you hadn't noticed, I am interested. I am calling dibs, but what if he doesn't play for our team?"

She laughed loudly. "Ha, I knew you were acting all weird, or at least weirder than usual, whenever we brought up the new guy's name. So that's why!"

"Do you think he's gay?" I asked earnestly.

"I am not just saying this because of your premature fantasies, but no, I didn't get that vibe when I met him earlier this week."

"Have you talked with him? What's he like?"

"Okay, slow down. I saw him in the storage room. I was getting branding material, and he was using the photocopier. I didn't get that much info, but even from that, he just seems like a nice guy. And he wasn't wearing a cardigan then."

"How do we find out? I don't want to make a fool of myself and start flirting to find out I have no chance."

"Seriously, Celeste, chill girl. We all work together, so I am sure there will be enough opportunity for you to test the waters."

"But what if my radar is off? I haven't dated in so long and for some reason I know I already like him, but what if I can't read the signs?"

Just then Simon opened the door to the office he shared with Sophie and smiled at us before heading to his desk. I gave Sophie a look that said: "I guess we'll have to finish this conversation another time." She laughed at me and shook her head.

Later that week, I ran into Dave in the photocopy room. It wasn't a promising setting for our first conversation. Because I supported the director of marketing, it's my role to check and replenish our brand stock, and that day the stock had arrived, giving me about ten huge, heavy boxes to place on the top shelf of the photocopy room. As I was standing on the counter in my stocking feet to place a box on the top shelf, in walked Dave. When I realized it was him, I was mortified. He could probably look up my dress from down there. Luckily, he kept walking by. I let out the breath I'd been holding.

Then, Dave circled back and asked if I needed some help. And there I stood on the counter in silence, not sure if it was for seconds or minutes. I kept repeating *breathe* in my mind until I eventually squeaked out, "That would be great." So, he passed me a box and I added it to the shelf, and we repeated this process until the rest of the boxes were shelved.

"Thank you," I said softly.

"No problem," he said curtly.

Then, he was gone. I had never had a problem talking before. How had I just wasted an opportunity to ask him questions about himself? It's practically my specialty. I groaned and slapped my forehead, then found Sophie and told her what had happened. I had no update about his sexual preferences.

"But Sophie, we still haven't figured out what team he plays for, and my imagination has been running wild about him. Do I have a chance here? Should I be flirting? Should I give up entirely? I feel so pathetic. Sophie, you must figure this out for me. I am relying on you. Otherwise, I might waste my efforts on someone I don't even have a chance with, and I could at least tell my stupid brain to stop daydreaming."

"What do you want me to do exactly? Shall I just go and ask him if he likes women?"

"No! But you could find out his relationship status, right? Oh crap, he could even be in a relationship. How have I not even thought about that yet? Here I am daydreaming of us riding off into the sunset and he might be engaged for all I know! I don't know what would be worse, him being gay or him being taken. Please, I am a pathetic mess and I need to know if I am wasting my time."

"Fine, but you owe me. You are getting my next three coffees."

CHAPTER 7 – DAVE

Christmas is around the corner, and I have always loved this time of year. It is the one time each year that life felt good at home. I grew up about an hour outside of Toronto, so there was always snow when I was little. Christmas break was full of snowball fights, snow forts, tobogganing, and waiting for Santa. My mum baked for weeks on end, the decorations were up, and everyone in the house was in a good mood. It was one of the only times my brothers and I got new things. It's not that we were poor, but we couldn't afford too many extras during the year, and Christmas made up for it. We got new clothes, toys, games, everything we asked for. We were spoiled rotten. Our whole year culminated at Christmas.

It was also a time when my dad lightened up when it came to discipline. Otherwise, he was always on us about something. It was the only attention we got from him growing up. Most days he didn't want anything to do with us, which suited us just fine. I try not to think about it too much, but it was an emotionally isolating way to grow up. Dad only started showing an interest in us once we were in our twenties. It's like he couldn't relate to children, so he didn't. To be completely honest, I don't even think he liked us. He was completely indifferent to our presence most days, and if we did attract his attention, it was not in our best interests. But a few pints and the promise of turkey would always lift his spirits, making Christmas one of the rare times we could all relax and be at ease.

This would be the first Christmas in three years with my parents. The holidays with my parents have really changed since I was little. Still lots of baking and presents, but now there is more beer and darts with my dad. Christmas as an adult is more about unplugging and forgetting about the daily-ness of life, rather than feeling the joy of the season. More than anything, I sleep, go for long walks with the dogs, and watch the Premier League. Honestly, though, I had thought I would be having Christmas with my own family by now and I'd be the one doing the baking, stirring the pudding, and decorating the tree. Creating my own traditions while carrying on the ones I grew up with as a child.

It makes me a bit sad starting over again, but leaving Jenn is a turning point for me. I'm not going to be trapped into settling for someone anymore. I know what I want and if it's not there, then I'll be content on my own. Though admittedly, the older I get, the further and further the possibility of a family is from being a reality. But maybe I still have time. Maybe I will meet someone. Maybe I'll stay on the island for an extra week or so, go down to Victoria and see what's there. Maybe, but more likely, I'll not even leave my parents' house other than for darts or dogs.

But Christmas is just over a month away, and in the interim, I have a townhouse to sell. Jenn, thankfully, spends most of her time at her mother's so that gives me enough time to get the place ready. This is a Vancouver market and your chances of coming out with extra is almost guaranteed, as long as you make sure the place looks top notch, so I ensure all the small details are looked after, such as cleaning the grout and tile of the mudroom with a toothbrush. I actually don't care that Jenn isn't helping because it means she isn't around and I don't have to talk to her. Things got pretty hostile once we decided to part ways, so she stays at her mom's most nights. My stomach would always sink when I came home and found her here. I can feel how angry she is at me. She doesn't understand why I ended things. But her anger has since subsided to the point where she doesn't care, which makes it clear we are making the right decision. I really want to get top dollar for the sale in Vancouver's hot real estate market because we will be splitting the profits and I need as much as I can get for my own down payment. I don't want to go back to renting again.

Before moving in with Jenn I lived in Kitsilano, which is the compulsory drop-off point for every Ontarian who moves to Vancouver, and I'm about a five minute walk from the beach. Since university, I had either roommates or lived with Deirdre. So, for the very first time, I'm completely on my own. I had been with Deirdre for so long, doing the things she liked to do, that I had completely forgotten who I was as an individual. I could not remember the things that I liked to do, so there was a bit of rediscovery. I rediscovered my love of Premier League football, my love of cooking, and I now had the time to revive old friendships. I also reacquired my love of nature, which Vancouver has in abundance. Nature is hard to find in Toronto, but if you look for it, you'll find it. I lived in Cabbagetown for three years, a few blocks from a huge dog park that leads into the Don Valley. I could walk for hours and hours with Tibby, under the viaduct all the way to the Brickworks. It was good, but Vancouver is on another level.

Tibby's my little angel. If I am being honest, she's probably the healthiest relationship I've ever been in. She's my first dog. I was lucky enough to get her for free out of the back of a pickup truck at a gas station. I answered an ad in a neighborhood paper and picked her up the next day. The last of an unwanted litter and meant for me. Tibby's part pure lab and part "lab/hound cross," according to the advert. Picture a skinny lab with really big ears. Way too big for her head. Now, rain or shine, which is mostly rain, we walk all over Point Grey for hours. Starting in the Endowment Lands, there are endless trails where Tibby can run off lead. Sometimes we walk along the seawall from Spanish Banks all the way down to Kits Beach if the tide is out. I feel fortunate every single day I wake up here.

The new job has been going fairly well so far. The people seem to be really welcoming. We'll see how long that lasts. My job has three primary functions: to identify new prospects for the capital campaign, to track the overall performance of the campaign, and to develop any new reporting required. That means tracking revenues and fundraisers. My job is, ideally, the bridge between the two main departments in any fundraising organization: Development (the fundraisers) and Operations (me). Eventually, my role of tracking fundraiser performance and the innate desire of all fundraisers to avoid being tracked makes for inevitable animosity between the two departments. But I'm used to it and it's relatively easy to find out who's doing what and who isn't.

For now, I'm figuring out the database, the campaign goals, and our performance to date. Thankfully, my boss has just let me get to work and skipped the whole meet and greet where I'm paraded around the office like some kind of pony. It's such a strange thing to do, but I've never understood office culture. For whatever reason, perfectly sane people come to the office as completely different people, totally devoid of any logical function and act as if they are in some kind of schoolyard. Bullying people, being passive-aggressive, or just plain acting out of character. I'm not saying everyone is like that; most are normal, but there are some who believe that because they have a particular title, they have superiority over others. Everyone is trapped in some form of cage, and whether it's a cubical or a corner office, it's still a cage. But for whatever reasons, those with the biggest cage believe they are special in some way, not recognizing that we are all in a cage. I'm no different. I'm a different person in the office, but not by choice. I always come in with an open attitude, but if someone wants to play schoolyard bullshit, I just ask them where the grownups are. Usually in a tone one uses when talking to children.

The staff in general seem okay, but I tend to stick to myself at work. Especially at the beginning of a new job. I arrive early and leave early so I don't get caught up in any after work drinks or whatever. Tibby is always my out if I need one, but it's best to avoid the conversation entirely if possible. I'd rather get to know people in a meeting and then decide if I should make any effort to get to know them. It saves time and prevents my exposure to idiocy. I'll eat lunch at my desk most days, but I'll often get cornered in the coffee room and have to make idle chitchat. I am usually aware enough to avoid anyone's interest in my presence, but coffee is my Achilles' heel and I unwittingly become rigid when I hear my name spoken behind me. Luckily, it's Sophie from Communications. I like Sophie. She's to the point as far as I can tell and isn't one for vacuous chatter.

"Hi. Dave, right? How are you settling in?"

"Hey, I'm good. Still finding my feet. My current challenge is to find where the coffee is kept."

Sophie gives me a brief tour of the office kitchen and we chat back and forth, easily and comfortably. I began to realize that I haven't really spoken to anyone other than my dog for quite some time. There were times since being on my own, that on a Monday morning, I realized that I had not uttered a word since I left work the previous Friday.

"So, what are you working on?" Sophie asks as she hands me the coffee grounds.

Ugh, preportioned coffee. "Just going through the database at the moment. Trying to find out if we have enough prospects to make our campaign goal. The numbers sort of make sense, but there isn't any activity on many of the accounts, so I'll have to look into that."

"Most of the fundraisers track activity in Excel."

"Really? Well, they won't be doing that for much longer. Anyway, I don't mind staying late for the next few weeks. Can't go home right after work anyway most days; too many viewings."

"Oh, you selling your place?"

"Yeah, can't wait for it to sell. It's a nice little townhouse. I owned it with my girlfriend, but it didn't work out, so we are selling. It's a bit awkward at the moment."

I have no idea why I suddenly opened up like that. I don't usually say anything to anyone, but there is something about Sophie. She's half German, half Mexican, but has lived in Vancouver most of her life. She's as tall as I am and still wears three-inch heels, which brings her up to about six-foot-four. I love that about her. She's open and receptive, yet simultaneously politely standoffish. Whatever it is, it's working for me, and I immediately feel comfortable around her. Sophie ends up being my connection to the rest of the staff.

One day we are all given a coupon for a free coffee and a few other people from the Communications team come by my desk to ask if I want to grab one. I don't have time to leave what I'm working on, but the rainbow tights girl says she can grab mine for me. Today's attire is some kind of bluish-purplish spacesuit with huge shoulder pads. It reminds me of the time my brother went to a Duran Duran concert in

'85, yet here we are in 2009. Go figure. I can't remember her name or maybe we have never been introduced, but I do remember her smile; it leaves an impression. Maybe I should find out her name.

CHAPTER 8 – CELESTE

I had no luck making conversation with Dave. He barely looked up from his computer no matter how many times I made excuses to walk by his cubicle. One day when I was wearing one of my favorite outfits because everything matched so well, my fitted dark purple dress with asymmetrical cut-out overlays paired with bright blue tights and my adorable black ankle booties and a pair of matching lightning bolt earrings, we asked him to join us to go get coffee, but he said he was too busy, so I offered to get his for him and he just said sure. I found out he took it black, but I wasn't sure how that information was helping me get to know him. I mean, I did get a little weird and tongue-tied in his presence, so it's not like he knew anything about me either. It made me think I was going to need to try a little harder to get his attention. He'd been working there for three weeks, and our only interaction had been the run-in in the photocopy room, not for a lack of passing his cubicle or constant trips to the washroom on his floor with the hope our paths would cross.

It's Monday, and I feel cute today. I'm wearing what I would call mod. Black blazer with high waisted pants and striped red-and-white blouse with some huge red hoops and matching red pumps. So, I give myself a mental pep talk: *Celeste, you got this, you're just saying hi. New week, new confident you.*

I check in with one of my directors and offer to take something to the CEO's office so I can walk by Dave's desk. On my way past his cubicle, I notice he has navy blue rain boots, and there's a cheese cutter hat sitting on his desk. Seriously, rain boots? Nothing makes me swoon more than rain gear. Trust me, we live in Vancouver and anyone who understands proper attire for the weather, well, oh my. I drop off the file folder with the CEO's assistant, Jade, another of my friends here in the office, and after some idle chitchat about our weekend plans, I make my way back to Dave's desk, putting my shoulders back and taking a deep breath.

I slow my walk and casually stop. Looking over toward Dave, I say, "I like your rain boots."

Dave looks straight ahead, staring at his computer screen. For a moment I don't know what to do. This is awkward, but I am just standing there, and I can't walk away without being acknowledged because then he will see me when I go to leave.

I try again a little louder. "Dave?"

Dave slowly looks up in my direction and almost jumps. "Oh, sorry, I didn't see you there. Did you say something?"

My cheeks burn red, and I repeat myself. "I like your rain boots."

Dave furrows his brows and tilts his head with an expression I can't make out. "Thanks, I guess."

Oh, this is not going well. I should probably introduce myself at least. "My name is Celeste. I don't think we ever got an introduction."

Dave gives me a lopsided smile and turns his head and body to face my direction. "Nice to meet you, Celeste. I'm Dave, but I think you already knew that, hence you just saying my name there."

I blurt out, "Yeah, technically when you were hired you were supposed to be introduced to every staff member on your first day, but for some reason, that didn't happen." I am drowning and alarm bells are going off in my head to evacuate. *Why would you say that? Get out of here, Celeste.*

Dave just shrugs and says, "Okay."

I give him my biggest smile, wave goodbye, and walk away. *Who am I? That was the most awkward conversation I have ever had. Why did I blurt that out? Why would he care or even need to know that I know we were never introduced?* I am never walking by his desk again or at least no more stopping, because apparently, I have lost my ability to communicate.

The rest of my Monday was pretty uneventful. I had more than enough to keep my thoughts occupied. There were always so many events at that time of year, and when you're admin for the director of events, that means you also support the whole team. So, it's all hands on deck. There were almost three events a week: some in-house happenings in the hospital and some evening ones at restaurants around the city. That Tuesday we had a press event to announce the completed funding for a brand-new MRI machine, and Wednesday we had a stewardship tea for an elderly care home.

The Events team were a well-oiled machine and knew exactly what they were doing. All arrangements made well in advance allowed for extra staff to show up and help set up and tear down. There was always a lot of energy buzzing, and it was fun to watch the good news flow. I enjoyed working there. I felt valued, and staff morale was high. I got along with all three of my directors and enjoyed being able to make them look good.

That's what I saw a good administrative assistant doing. If you supported your boss effectively, they would always come across as competent, organized, and punctual. You did all the heavy lifting in the details so that when they spoke and shared their expertise, they shone.

The week goes by in a blur, which helps keep my mind from thinking about Dave. I wasn't in the office much with all the events and it looks like his role and mine don't really overlap. On Friday, Sophie pops her head in my office. "Hey, you want grab me one of those coffees?"

I have a huge smile on my face. "You got details?"

Sophie just grins at me and nods toward the exit. I grab my purse and out of the office we head, making our way down the stairs to the open hallway that leads to the other side of the hospital and the new Starbucks. Going to Starbucks in Vancouver is kind of an institution itself. I mean, they even have competing locations across the street from each other.

Once we are alone walking through the hospital, I will myself to be calm and whisper. "Did you get any intel?"

Sophie nods. "Yes, I was in the kitchen, and he needed help finding the coffee. We ended up chatting."

"And?"

Sophie laughs, getting a kick out of this and trying to draw it out. "Well, he told me he is currently getting his townhouse ready to sell."

I glare at her. "And?"

"Well, he owns it with his girlfriend."

My face instantly drops, and I stare at my feet while slowly shuffling forward. Well, that's the end of that. Back to eHarmony, I guess. Why do I feel almost nauseated from the news? It's not like I have even talked to him. I mean, he could be a total dork and completely annoying. *Yeah, keep telling yourself that, Celeste; whatever you need to say to get over this stupid fantasy.*

Sophie continues with a wide grin. "But they are selling it because they just broke up and will be going their separate ways."

I stop her and grab her shoulders. "Are you kidding with me?"

She just smiles.

"So, what you are telling me is, first, we know he likes women, and second, he is recently single!" My chest is about to explode with hope and excitement. I have whiplash from the 180 that just happened. Forget what I said about being dorky and annoying. We know he is smart, smooth, and smoldering.

Sophie grabs me by the shoulders and turns my body to start walking again. "That's right, now let's get me my coffee."

"Whatever you want. You are simply the best and deserve it all!" I swing my arms through hers and almost skip us all the way to Starbucks.

The afternoon goes by in a daze as my daydreaming takes on a new level. I mean, I need to get back to reality. This guy barely knows I exist, and so far, our communication has been dismal and awkward. Why do I do this to myself? Imagine something that isn't even there—or is it? Okay, great, I now know he likes women, but it doesn't mean he will like me. Who am I kidding? It's almost like it was better before I knew because I could pretend. Now, if I get rejected, it will be because of me. It's like this new information has just sent me down my own self-confidence spiral again.

My walk home is a serene twenty minutes, and I love it; it always helps calm my racing mind. I feel like the weather gods made clear skies to help lift my spirits and distract me from my spiraling thoughts. Walking along 10th Avenue is my favorite part of the day. Sometimes I'll pop into a bookstore or a clothing boutique on the way home and enjoy the feeling of not being in a rush and being able to see the skyline of the city with the mountains beyond. I truly do love this city, and the walk helps to clear my mind.

The smell of the sweet salty air and fresh rain makes me feel lucky to be alive. Maybe I just need to let go of this fantasy I have created and get back to basics. Time to focus on what to have for dinner, and these days, that is mostly either mac and cheese or a can of beans. But even though I might not have much money for food, it's still better than making a meal from scratch for someone who doesn't even care how much effort I put into it. It feels good not to think about Mike, who is already like a distant memory.

CHAPTER 9 – DAVE

I have my first meeting with some of the senior leadership about the current capital campaign. I've been doing this kind of work for long enough that, after going over the numbers for the last few weeks, I know it's going to be a difficult meeting. The nonprofit sector is probably one of the most loosely regulated sectors I can think of. Sure, financially, they are audited annually. The money coming in and going out is always in sync, but it's my job to look forward and focus on forecasting future revenues. In addition to being the bridge between the Operations and Fundraising departments, I also act as a bridge between the IT department and the fundraisers. Well, more like a translator than a bridge. The databases never "worked" for fundraisers, so they would manage everything in Excel, which was a nightmare because they all did it differently and, in my experience, often fabricated data based on fantasies they told themselves. The IT departments, for their part, couldn't make the database "work" because the fundraisers lacked the ability to articulate what they needed, so the IT folks had to cobble something together based on what they were instructed, which would inevitably end up not working for either party. That's where I came in. I would interpret what the fundraisers needed and either relay that to IT or, because I knew just enough about database management that what the fundraisers wanted was not possible due to the logical constraints of the system they were using, IT wouldn't have to be involved in the process at all.

I was an English literature major in university. I did my master's program studying Keats' poetry, so I have no idea how I ended up doing this type of work. Like everyone else, I guess I just needed to find work after graduation. I didn't have another six years in me to complete a PhD, so I went for a master's degree in library science. I wanted initially to be an academic librarian and focus on research best practices, collection development and the like, but to cover my bases, I decided to add database management and design. The latter was much more useful as my career moved forward, though I really hated it. Over the years I've taken courses and received certification in Data Analytics, Visualization, and Report Development. I get my Tableau certification updated every year, and in this place, they've even got me coding in SQL. All the while hating every single moment of it. If I could turn back the clock, I never would have pursued this kind of work. I'd have done anything that got me outside. *"Places of nestling green for poets made."*

I loved my time at university. It was a six-year bubble when I didn't have to care about the outside world. I took courses on different forms of literature, reading novels, books of poetry, and the literary theory that accompanied them. I took supplementary courses in history and comparative literature, which was a unique way of looking at literature through different lenses of history, music, and politics from varying cultures, seeing how they intertwined and developed. I had some amazing professors. The best were the ones who had tenure and didn't have the unbearable pressures of constantly having to publish. They could focus solely on teaching. They loved doing it and it showed. They were able to simply pass their knowledge to a younger generation and see the wonder of discovery on faces like mine, devouring beautifully told stories and the context in which they were written. It was such a wonderful time. Now, ten years later, I find myself in a box under fluorescent lights trying to explain to people who don't understand anything about databases why recording everything in Excel is not in anyone's best interest.

Fundraisers are a bit of an odd group in that many have no idea what they are doing. They come from various backgrounds, which is fine, but for some reason, they don't believe they need any kind of supplemental knowledge in order to understand their role and keep up to date with changes within the industry. Not all of them, but a significant number have absolutely no idea how to manage a capital campaign, especially ones in the hundreds of millions like this one. There's no real educational background needed to become a fundraiser. Sales, business, or finance would be helpful, but the irony is that fundraisers refuse to look at themselves as salespeople, which is exactly the type of personality needed in a role like this, someone who can pitch large-scale visions to potential donors. They prefer to see themselves as something more noble, as if they themselves are performing some act of philanthropy by taking on the moral mission of fundraising. The eventual animosity that happens between fundraisers and those charged with actually managing the numbers is due to one being based on the information presented and the other being based on the imaginings of "maybes."

The meeting today is an attempt to get some clarity on the current status of our campaign. First thing is to find out how many prospects we have and make sure it comes close to matching our fundraising targets.

I have handed out photocopies to all attendees that show what we are going to talk about, basically, what the database is currently showing me. There are seven of us in the boardroom on the main floor.

"So, I've been going through the database, and I was hoping to go through some of your assigned prospects and get some updates. Bill, it looks as though you have over five hundred prospects currently in solicitation, but there is no activity on the records. What is your strategy for these constituents?"

After a moment, Bill replies, "Oh, those are placeholders."

"For what?"

With a bit of snark, Bill responds, "For a donation."

I am trying to be patient. "To what?"

"To the campaign."

I know he is trying to be clever, but I stay calm in my responses. "But according to the system, there's no indication that you have ever spoken to them."

Bill rolls his eyes. "No, I haven't, yet. They are placeholders so we don't forget about them."

"Some of these entries are over seven years old."

"So those prospects we will have to take a look at again," Bill says.

I really do need to get some answers in order for me to do my job correctly, so I have to ask, "But how did they get here in the first place? Why are they here?"

Bill replies with blatant sarcasm. "They have money."

Again, I remain calm. "Yes, they do. But what makes you consider them a good prospect for this campaign?"

Bill is not budging. "They have money."

Aw crap. I've been here before. He doesn't understand what I'm talking about, and for the first time in this guy's long and unaccountable career, he comes up against someone who is asking direct questions about where he's getting his numbers. Bill's not bothered. I'm just some clown two to three pay grades below him, asking questions that he feels he doesn't have to answer and no one can make him. The whole thing is so childish. *Shit. Well, let's see what I'm working with here.*

I try again, so everyone in the room can clearly understand my reasoning. "So, we have over five hundred prospects that have had your placeholder for future engagement for the past seven years. We have no idea why they are in the system. We don't know if they are connected to us in any way, and many have never even made a donation to us before. Is it safe to assume that this placeholder system that you created isn't working?"

Many attendees in the meeting start awkwardly shifting in their seats. Apparently, no one has spoken like this to Bill before. I scan the faces at the table. There are a few admin staff there for support, their eyes wide. The senior vice president, on the right, looks to be seething and quietly wishing me dead. The director of development, on the left, is similar to Bill. Both have been here for decades, and both are confused as to why someone would choose to speak to them in this manner. The president of the foundation is there; he seems somewhat interested in the answer, but only out of curiosity, and this is where I kind of need him to step in so I can get some answers, but he's not. This is their campaign, and the new guy is telling them straight out that their prospects are garbage, at least according to the database, and that's not good. My boss is definitely interested in the answer, but he's waiting to see how I handle the situation.

No one in this room knows these prospects, who they are or why they are here, but notes have been taken, spreadsheets distributed, and supplementary meetings booked. The setup is destined to fail and for the rest of my tenure here, I will be fighting with these people to make any type of change, despite the clear need for change this meeting displayed. The changes I need them to make are boring and tedious, I get that. It requires them entering a ton of data on a regular basis, adding new entries, modifying existing procedures, and designing new reports. It is boring work and it's not for everyone, but I'll be the one doing all the work. All they have to do is enter their activity logs, that's it, but they refuse to do it. They seem to think it's beneath them, that it takes time away from fundraising. But this *is* fundraising. It's the most important part and they refuse to do it, but with no accountability as to whether or not they do it, why would they?

What usually happens at this point is that I end up coordinating with the admin assistants to see how all this is really done. If it's like every other place I've worked in, they are the ones entering the activity logs for their respective teams and are more than happy to enter the data into the system. I design all my data entry programs to be easier to do than the current method. The admin staff are always charged with the execution of the finer details within the organization, so if I can make their lives easier, then they have no problems making the changes.

Later, I find out we have an upcoming fundraising gala, so I send out some emails to the Events team to see who is running it. Communication and Events departments are good in this industry because they actually want to keep track of everything, so they are up next. There are a few people in the Communications department who seem nice, and they swing by my cubicle a few times a week, asking if I want to get coffee with them. Sometimes I am just too focused and can't take a break, and sometimes I don't even hear them because I'm deaf in my left ear so people stop by and I don't realize they asked me for anything because I don't hear them.

Rainbow Tights came by my desk and gave me the oddest compliment. "I like your rain boots." Who compliments people on their choice of footwear? And if you are going to acknowledge them, at least call them Wellies, not rain boots. These aren't from Home Depot. Dad always said if you're going to move to the coast, best to buy "proper Wellingtons," so the last time we went to England I picked up some Hunters at the local Cornwall Farmers. It's nice to finally be able to use them.

I was born in Canada, but you could never tell my parents I'm not English. As far as they were concerned, they were an English couple raising their English children in a British colony. I don't know how many times at dinner Mum would say, "Canadians are so stupid."

"I'm Canadian, Mum."

"No, you're not."

"I was born in Toronto. Doesn't sound like an English town to me."

"Well, you are not."

Suffice to say, I grew up in "an English household" despite any protestations. My parents moved to Canada in '67, coinciding with a mass migration to Canada from the UK at that time. Despite all the other expats, it always was just the five of us (I have two older brothers). My parents were either not interested in or had a very difficult time making friends. We never went anywhere and never really had anyone over. I used to envy the other kids talking about their families at holidays. They would talk about visiting aunts, uncles, and cousins, or having grandparents over for dinner, but we never had that.

The stereotypes regarding the English having a "stiff upper lip" and all that are true to some extent. It's definitely the way I grew up.

I didn't know it at the time, but it was a strange environment to grow up in. It felt misplaced and out of date. When I met other English families, or my relatives in England, they were much more jovial, more relaxed, and much happier than mine, so the stereotype only seemed to reflect my family. My parents manifested right out of a Victorian era novel, Dickens in particular. There were no pleasantries, no "good mornings" nor "How was your day?" It was a house devoid of any emotion. My parents never laid a hand on us other than for disciplinary purposes: we were never hugged, never kissed, never were the words "I love you" uttered within the house, even when we were children. I don't know why. My mum's love language was acts of service: cooking, cleaning, looking after everyone, and I continued that pattern as I grew up. My dad was an emotionless narcissist, devoid of any feeling toward any other human being. I also continued that pattern to some extent. But I had lots of friends, and they made up for the lack of affection at home.

As a kid, I would come home to nothing but a set of instructions on how to get dinner started: peel this, mash that, grate, chop, whatever needed to get dinner on the table by the time Mum got home. My mum worked shift work at the police station, so sometimes she was home and sometimes not, but as long as there was a note, I was good to go as far as taking care of myself. Even if I didn't have to do anything, Mum would always leave a note to let me know what time she would be home.

Once, when I was about seven or so, I came home and there was no note for me. I waited for a while and then I thought: *I know, I'll call Mummy's work.* But when I called the police station and she wasn't there, they started asking questions like "Who's your Mommy, sweetheart?" and "Are you on your own?" Once they found out who my mum was, they sent a cruiser over. When my mum came home, she found me sitting at the kitchen table with the constable. I had made him coffee.

"Hi, Kenny."

"Hello, Barbara, how are you?"

"Good, thanks, but the car broke down. Thanks for looking after Dave."

Kenny was a great guy. He made the best cakes. One time, for my birthday, he made a Beatles cake for me. Dark chocolate with grooves on the top like an LP and a candy circle in the middle with all the songs written out from the *For Sale* album, with little plastic Beatles figures playing their instruments on top. It was wonderful.

After that pointless thought shower with senior leadership, I don't have it in me to do any more work, so I prep myself for the following day, then head to the pub to meet Paul and try and shake that whole thing off. I'll take a little more casual approach for tomorrow's meeting with Communications. This ain't Toronto, and Vancouver isn't responding to the direct approach. Maybe I'll buy them all a coffee tomorrow and make it informal. Paul and I meet at the Three Lions on Broadway at five sharp. Librarians are never late, and Paul and I went to school together and have kept in touch ever since. He's at the university, but he still understands the general frustrations of our profession, so it's a good way to blow off steam.

"What are you having?"

"Sour Cherry Stout."

I grimace. "Why do you drink that crap?"

"There's more to beer than lager."

"Yeah, Ales and Bitters." I turn to the waiter. "Pint of Bitter, please."

"How's the new job going?"

"It's good. Me and my boss get along really well. We seem to get each other, and he's given me some room to figure stuff out on my own. And I've started to meet some people in other departments, mostly Communications: Sophie, Celeste, and Simon so far. I meet with that team tomorrow. I met with the fundraisers today."

"How did that go?"

"Same as usual. 'We need someone to help us develop new reports so we can stay on top of our campaign.' So, I gave them the usual spiel on how to do things properly and they all agreed that they weren't going to do that. So, it will be a long slough."

I go into a bit more detail about the day, but not too much. I am trying to enjoy myself. Paul has his own venting to do. He works for a research department in the faculty of medicine and gripes on how each regional, provincial, and federal institution tracks data differently and the majority of his job is cramming all of it into something that is useful. It seems the majority of administrative professions like ours are not much more than tidying up other people's messes. None of us signed up for this.

"How are things going with the sale?"

"Have two more viewings tonight and one isn't until six, so I'm going to grab something to eat here. I don't mind the interest, but I can't keep eating out all the time. It's getting too expensive." The waiter passes by our table and I add, "Yes, another pint, please. Thanks."

"Any offers?" Paul asks.

"Both of tonight's viewings are second viewings, so hopefully I hear something soon."

"Is Jenn still staying at her mom's?"

"As far as I can tell. We both just want this to end. But if we get the price we are asking, we will both walk away with about twenty grand. That should be enough to put a down payment on something."

"Maybe."

It isn't raining so I walk home. It takes about thirty minutes, but there's no rush to get there. I turn onto Arbutus, a few blocks south, then up the stairs. There are lights on. I hold my breath, turn the key, and open the door. Tibby greets me, but no Wally. Jenn's not home.

I find the older I get, the more I need to maintain my routine. It keeps me sane. It's probably why, as much as I find my job frustrating, I still do it. I like things in order. I like things in their proper place so it's easier to find them later. This makes perfect sense to me and apparently very little sense to others. Hence the frustrations of my job. I get up every day at five. I have two cups of coffee. Get dressed and take Tibby out. This morning, I wear a fleece, full rain suit, and Wellies, but in the summer, it's flip-flops, T-shirts, and shorts. I miss summer. Watching the sunrise in the morning, and in the evening, I dump some ice in a Safeway bag with a couple of cans, Tibby and I head down to the dog beach, and we watch the sunset on the water. It washes every care away. No matter what kind of day I've had, I am reminded that none of that really matters, and I simply sit in the beauty of things: "*A thing of beauty is a joy forever; its loveliness increases; it will never pass into nothingness.*"

However, this is December, so into the darkness we walk. It's raining pretty hard when we arrive at Kits Beach Park, and we're all alone. I let Tibby off lead, relax, and let my mind wander. We had multiple bids on our place last night and got about 10 percent over ask from one buyer. The only big condition they had was a fast closing date. Jenn and I will have no problem with that. *I need to find an apartment quickly.*

I'll have enough to put a down payment on a decent place here in Kits and may even have enough to buy a car. Ever since this relationship turned sour, I've been actively turning my mind toward a future without a family, and it is not looking too bad. I kind of knew this was my last chance and was having a hard time letting it go, but I'm getting there. I have images of Tibby and me driving down the Pacific coast to Washington, then Oregon, then California. My mum and dad drove down to Carmel last summer and said it was incredibly dog friendly. I've started looking at maps and realizing how much there is to see. We could even go to Nevada or the Arizona desert. I've always wanted to see that, and I would have the time. I could leave Tibby with my parents and go to England again to do some more hiking there; maybe the Yorkshire Dales this time.

I let my mind meander through all the different possibilities. They feel good. We walk past the tennis courts and playground, through Hadden Park, then pass in front of the Maritime Museum. As we walk through Vanier Park and its little pond, I keep my eyes open for coyotes. They like to snatch ducks by the water's edge. Tibby wanders but always stays pretty close. When she was younger, she kept taking off and not coming back. I had a little light on her collar so I could know where she was going, but all it did was make me aware of how far away she was. It wasn't until the following spring and the days getting lighter that I realized she had been chasing coyotes all morning. So, now I keep her close. We turn back at the Coast Guard station, walking through Vanier Park along the water's edge, then Kits Beach and back home. The whole walk takes about an hour round trip. Then it's to Kitsilano Community Centre to work out, then back home to eat, shower, and get dressed. I'm usually in the office by 7:30.

The Christmas decorations are up, and everyone seems to be feeling the spirit of the season. I feel good. It's going to be a good day. I am meeting with the Communications team this morning. I decide to keep it casual so instead of a formal meeting, I head upstairs to see if anyone wants to grab a coffee and ask them a few questions on the way to see how they manage their information. I pop my head into Sophie's office. She says to give her a moment to see if anyone else wants to join us and as I back out of her office to wait in the hallway, someone slams right into my back so hard that I even stumble a little. Before I can utter a tirade of profanity, I see it's Celeste and she is sitting on her ass on the floor rubbing her head. Looks like she got it worse than me.

I quickly reach my hand down to help her up. "You okay?"

"Oh, thank you, yes. I'm so sorry I just ran into you. I wasn't looking and had my head down. Usually, the path is clear. I am so sorry."

As she reaches for my hand, her cheeks flush, and she looks up at me with a bright smile. I remember that smile from before. It does something to me. I don't really know what I would call it because it's such an unfamiliar feeling, but my chest feels warm. Celeste stands and lets go of my hand. I feel her hand's absence and the warmth in my chest starts to subside. "It's all right. I just came to ask if Sophie wanted to get a coffee. You guys all seem to have a thing for that here." *You don't have to try to be clever every minute of every day, Dave. Just try to make some friends without sounding like a jackass.*

"Sounds good. I haven't had my coffee yet. I don't have a maker at home anymore, so I wait until I come into the office." Just then,

Sophie comes out of her office with Simon. I'm curious to know what Celeste means by "anymore," but we all leave through the back doors, down the stairs, and across the lobby. I am surprised that over a third of the Communications team can leave the office without anyone noticing, but although we do work in a hospital, no lives will be lost in our departure.

Celeste and Simon are walking in front of Sophie and me. Sophie is talking about something she did on the weekend, but I am not really listening because I am fascinated by Celeste's outfit. Looks like we are in preschool today and I am being led by our teacher on our field trip to Starbucks. It's a full body bright green tunic with argyle leggings. I guess the rainbow tights are in the wash. To be fair, the legs beneath those leggings are long and athletic, it's just hard to see past the retina-burning colors of the leggings. However, I appreciate the ability to be bold. No one would ever call me bold in any aspect of my life, especially when it comes to fashion. When my brother got his promotion at the bank, he only had two suits. On the elevator, someone asked him if he was Einstein. Apparently, Albert Einstein had seven variations of the same clothes so he wouldn't have to exert any "decision fatigue" into what he was going to wear. My brother took offense to this. I, on the other hand, ran with it and bought five identical white dress shirts, three wool sweaters (gray/blue/black), and two pairs of dress pants and whatever number of ties I had picked up over the years. Was it boring? Yes. Was it efficient? Also yes. Celeste definitely has the personality to go with her outfits, though. She is regularly in a good mood and eager to help. She's bright. Sparkling bright.

We all get to Starbucks and I decide to treat them because it was my idea, and everyone seems genuinely thankful. Such a different atmosphere from yesterday's meeting. Well, except for that Simon guy, who keeps giving me the side-eye. I wonder if he and Celeste have a thing.

I get back to my desk and look at my inbox. I am already behind for the day. Ugh, this is why I don't do these coffee runs. I have too much to do and now I'll have to play catch up for the rest of the day. I did enjoy going, though. Felt good.

CHAPTER 10 – CELESTE

Well, that was an unexpected surprise this morning. My favorite part was when I accidently ran straight into Dave because it forced my nose into his back and I got the most delightful treat. I got to smell him. Yep, looked like I wasn't being cool again. But how could I remain cool after smelling him into my soul? Seriously, he smelled of a foresty musk with a hint of sea salt. But it was more than that; it was like I knew this smell, like this smell was something familiar and comforting. It had a hint of pepper, and the strength of it did something that made my legs feel all tingly.

Yes, that had been embarrassing, but then he took my hand, and it was so soft, yet firm and commanding at the same time. It felt like my hand belonged in his. My imagination ran away with me. But I swear, it was the first time he noticed me, and it was almost like I could feel his eyes on me while we walked to get coffee. I wish I knew what he was thinking. I savored that coffee and was in the best mood because I learned he was kind and thoughtful. My list came to mind like a big billboard and started highlighting some of my wants: Big smile, white teeth, and kind. Check, Check, Check.

Our work Christmas party was coming up at the end of the week, and because I was part of the planning committee, I thought I could find a way for us to sit at the same table. Maybe I'd have the chance to get another whiff of him, and perhaps even an opportunity to talk with him. Christmas always put people in a good mood. It's a great way to move people out of work mode and gave us all an opportunity to get to know each other on a social level. Even though it's just a few hours on a Friday afternoon, who didn't like to enjoy themselves a little?

My memories of Christmas have always been conflicting for me, though. My most memorable moments are from my childhood and being spoiled rotten by my nana and papa. Theirs was the only place where candy and treats flowed while I watched *Pink Panther* and *Inspector Gadget* with my brother. One of my mom's parental rules had always been no sweets or TV. She made ice cream by hand, and canned fruit was the only option for dessert. When I was young, she convinced me that parsley was gum. She went into the yard, grabbed a bunch of parsley, and literally told me to chew it. She knew what my imagination was capable of. So, at Nana and Papa's house, we were spoiled, and we loved it. Sugar and TV as much as we could handle, the complete opposite world of my daily life. Visiting my grandparents was like visiting Disneyland, as far as I was concerned. My papa had been in the Navy and had been tough on my dad, but his grandkids could do no wrong. He made us hot chocolate with four teaspoons of sugar, and my aunt often brought us Twinkies and rocket candies. On trips to McDonald's with my brother and cousin, Papa would have us all singing. Some of my favorite memories are those early years.

But the "golden years" got crushed when the divorce happened. My stepmom wasn't a fan of my grandparents' smoky house and had no connection to our traditions. My mom even tried to take us there for a few years. Her time with us started on Christmas at noon, and one year we drove to the island from the Okanagan. Even though these weren't my mom's parents, they had known her since she was sixteen, and these moments mattered to all of us. However, over the years we stopped visiting as often, and Christmas turned a bit sad for me. Christmas Eve and morning at my dad's were fine and then

Mom picked us up in the afternoon and the three of us hung out. I think that's why when I started having boyfriends, I spent the holiday with them and their families. By the time I moved away, I didn't have much of an allegiance to anywhere. I didn't feel like I belonged in any home. Therefore, in the years of dating Mike, I loved going to his home and being a part of his traditions. I could always count on lots of happy family activity and celebration. It reminded me of the wonder and promise of Christmas that I'd loved as a child with my grandparents.

It is now Friday and as part of the planning committee, I leave work early to go set up at the Jericho Yacht Club. Every Christmas our foundation has a standing date to have our party here, and I love it. It is such a treat because when you live in such a beautiful city, but you're broke, you feel really fortunate to get to experience Vancouver opulence.

Sophie, Jade, and I unload the vehicles and start unpacking all the Christmas presents and prizes to give out and games to be played. Everyone will sit at one of the six tables. My idea of assigned seating was outvoted, which meant I couldn't arrange to sit on Dave's lap, I mean, at the same table. So, I volunteered to stand at the front door holding the stocking, where everyone would randomly pull out a number that assigned them a table. This would give me the opportunity to welcome everyone, which would include Dave.

I made sure to wear an outfit that makes me feel confident: tight black jeans, brown riding boots, and my teal off-the-shoulder sweater. This outfit is more sophisticated and subdued compared to the pops of color I typically wear. I like bright colors because every shade of the rainbow makes me happy. I think I am the only person who had moved to Vancouver who didn't live in black or gray clothing.

The committee has finished setup, and almost everyone has arrived, except Dave. Then, I see him walking down the stairs and he stops. We look at each other and time stands still, but I am sure it is just a few seconds. He hangs up his coat in the closet and slowly makes his way down the hall toward me. I hold my breath and my lady bits do a little holding themselves. He is so handsome, tall, and fit, and just right. He has these soft curls, which make me want to run my fingers through them, and his walk is purposeful. Seriously, how does this man walking toward me make me swoon just by his gait?

He then stands in front of me with a little smile on his face and I notice his lips. How had I not noticed them before? He has full lips, top and bottom, and they look soft. *Oh, stop staring at his lips!* I then look up into his eyes and almost melt on the spot. I swear his moss green eyes have twinkle lights of gold strung throughout. The centers of his eyes are like caramel sparks that have leaked to the edges where they blend into a sea of green. Man, if I was in trouble before, I'm a goner now! My daydreaming ends when Dave says, "Hi, Celeste, am I supposed to get something from you?"

I am having trouble forming words. Dave tries again, lifting his shoulders. "Do I just go inside?"

I squeak out, "Ah, yeah, reach into my bag and pull out a number and that number corresponds to the table where you sit."

Dave chuckles, which I can only imagine is at my lack of communication skills. He takes his time reaching in the bag, pulls out a number, and we both look down. He's at table four. My smile falls and Dave heads toward his table, which is across the room from mine. *Just great!*

So, I realize I need to get creative to find ways to get into Dave's vicinity. Now that I know how he smells, I need another inhale, and his eyes, oh how I could get lost in his stargazing eyes. And those lips! I would die happy if I got to kiss those lips even just once. So, I march over to Simon and offer to take the work camera and photograph the party. This will give me an excuse to circulate.

Simon and I have always gotten along really well. We have a firm sibling bond, except sometimes I don't know if he sees it in the same way. Ever since Simon joined the Communications team two years ago, it's been Simon, Sophie, and me. We have daily coffees and hang out the occasional weekend. However, ever since Dave started and we have been inviting him along, Simon's demeanor has changed a little. I haven't overtly told him I am interested in Dave, but I think he can tell that my attention is now on someone else. In the past few weeks, he has almost gotten snippy with me. So, when I ask if I can take photos, he just hands over the department's camera and says, "Have at it."

But I'm terrible at taking photos! I *love* taking them, but what I try to capture and what I see on the photo screen are very different. Good thing everyone is more concerned about getting free drinks and an afternoon off from work. I move from table to table taking photos as everyone gets seated and acquainted with others at their table. Everyone is asked to create a funny team name that will then be used for the future games our committee planned. I sidle up behind Dave, acting like I am getting a photo over his shoulder of the center of their table, only to try and breathe in his scent. Yep, it's amazing and makes me almost fall over. Maybe if I did, Dave would catch me, and we would ride into the sunset with his pillow-soft lips and—

"Celeste?"

Shit! How long have I been standing behind Dave? The camera isn't even poised in front of my face; it's by my hip as I lean behind Dave's shoulder like a weirdo. Oh, I hope he didn't hear me inhale him. I grab the camera and try to act casual. "Ah, I'm on camera duty and am just getting some team photos. I think I've got a bunch of your table, so . . . um, great. See you later."

Dave must think I am nuts, if he didn't already.

CHAPTER 11 – DAVE

My boss pops his head into my office. "I have some things to finish up, but if you want to wait a bit, I can drive you."

"Sure. That'd be great, thanks."

I don't know why I'm feeling so stressed. Today is the Christmas party, but all I can think of is how I have to cram a day's work into half a day. I don't know why I do this to myself. No one else seems to care. In fact, I'm pretty sure everyone else is gone except our team.

We pile into my boss's car and head to the yacht club. I am liking the Operations Team. There are five of us and whether by design or not, we are all very straightforward and feel comfortable with each other. I think it's my boss's doing. He's originally from Vancouver but spent the majority of his career in Toronto, as well as at some big institutions in the States. He's very well respected, and to be honest, I am a bit confused why he is in, by comparison, such a small fundraising shop. Apparently, he's old friends with the president and was hired to take the foundation in a particular direction. We hit it off immediately, and so far, things are going very well. Our group consists primarily of administrative, finance, and data management. So, all socially awkward, but we play well together under specific conditions. Today was one of those conditions. As soon as we drive away, Lena from Finance blurts out confidently, "So after lunch, do we have to come back to the office?"

Though I already had plans to evaporate shortly after lunch, I mentally thank her for asking that question. I have no intention of going back to the office after multiple pints.

"Well," my boss responds, "I'm not going to be coming back to the office after, so I would have no idea as to whether or not you returned."

And with that, the afternoon became much brighter despite the impending rain. It's always better to get permission to take off in the afternoon.

The party is at the Jericho Yacht Club. While the others walk right in, I give myself a little tour of the grounds. Vancouverites are used to the scenery, but not me. The club is right on the water, looking across English Bay to West Vancouver and the North Shore Mountains. It's beautiful. After a few minutes, I walk in, head down the stairs, and take my coat off. At the end of the long hallway is Celeste. She looks different. She's wearing black jeans and a green top. Maybe it's because this outfit isn't burning my retinas, but it's like I'm seeing her for the first time. Her dark brown hair falls just above her shoulders. Tall and slim, she stands perfectly still and beams a smile at me. I stand there, staring back, not sure for how long. I walk toward her, all the while looking at her face. Celeste has dark brown eyes that almost pull me down the hall. Her face is a perfect oval, with a beautiful jawline that draws the eye down to her gracefully slender neck, which, like the stem of a flower, continues into the green of her sweater.

She holds a small bag. I put my hand in and take out my table number, never taking my eyes off Celeste. I'm not entirely sure what's happening, but something definitely is. I walk into the banquet hall and face a wall of windows across the west face of the building. The sea is calm, but the clouds have darkened, and it is starting to rain. The hall has a nautical theme with blue and cream-colored bead board with wood beamed ceilings. Beautiful.

Like a moth to a flame, I move toward the bar. After securing a pint of Phillips, I scan the room for someone on the Operations Team I can talk to. I've never been good at mingling and need a mediary to see me through the process. To anyone new, I come across as somewhat indifferent, which I think upsets people, either consciously or unconsciously. Add to this my apathy for their discomfort, et voilà, cumbersome. I am making a concerted effort to change, yet simultaneously, I don't really care if I do. I see Sophie talking to a small group at one of the tables and decide that's my best entry point. I smile and wish everyone a Merry Christmas as I scan the room for Celeste. I see her by the door, guiding people to their tables, answering questions, and being generally helpful. Everyone seems to like Celeste, which is no mystery as her enjoyment in helping others is genuine. I watch her walk about the room, smiling and laughing with others, gently touching their arm or shoulder, spreading her light throughout the space.

"I'm sorry, what?"

"I said, I heard you used to work at the Vancouver Foundation. Do you know Suzanne?"

Suzanne? Who is Suzanne? Who are you for that matter? Crap. Did I say that out loud? Her face says no, so that was my inside voice.

"I don't think so. I was only there for a year," I say, still attempting to figure out who this person is speaking to me.

We continued talking for a minute or two. She seems nice, but I have no idea who she is, and for the first time in my life, I am wishing everyone had name tags. My apathy kicks in and I let go of my interest in determining this person's name and resume my search for Celeste. I can't seem to find her, and this conversation is breaking down rapidly, so I make an excuse to find my table. There's a sheet on each one with a list of upcoming team-building activities. If they just called them games, I wouldn't have such a visceral aversion to them. I know the purpose is to have us interact and to feel more comfortable with each other, but that's what my second pint is for. I scan the games and they actually look like they could be fun. We need to come up with a team name. There's lots of ways to play this, but I don't know these people very well and decide to keep it clean. "How about the Fund Razors?" I say. Just enough combination of corny and clever. They didn't think so and we go with Team Tinsel. I usually don't really care enough to say anything, so I am proud of myself for my contribution.

I have no luck finding Celeste when I suddenly realize she's standing right behind me. She is staring far off into the distance, lost in thought. Wherever she went, it looked like a pleasant place. "Celeste?" She immediately pops back into reality. She is on camera duty for the party and is taking pictures. She mutters a few words and continues to move around the room. She's piqued my curiosity. There is a sincerity about her, an authenticity I can't quite describe, but I have fallen into a complete fascination with her.

The lunch is really good, the conversation is easy, and I find myself relaxing a bit. After some small talk with a coffee in hand, it's time to start the team-building portion of the afternoon. My old self would find any excuse I could to jettison myself and get out of here, but for some reason, I actually want to work here and getting to know my coworkers and showing a bit of my personality will probably help me in the office. My role itself is one I take very seriously, so it's probably a good idea for me to make an effort to get to know these people. Maybe it would balance out my direct approach in meetings so they can see I have a sense of humor and can enjoy the simple things at times.

The first game is a version of Pictionary that has been taken from another game called Cranium. We pull our chairs into a semi-circle around a big white board, where Celeste stands front and center. She goes over the rules with everyone. Telling everyone how to play this game seems to light her up. We play a few rounds. My table loses miserably, and Celeste's team cleans up. After a few more rounds and some other games, most of the senior staff decide to excuse themselves. The CEO tells all of us that no one needs to go back to the office and the afternoon is ours. I start contemplating what I will do with some free time this afternoon. I do have a bit more Christmas shopping to do, and Tibby would also be pretty excited to see me get home early, but when I look outside and see the weather, it's absolutely pouring. These are the moments I wish I had someone in my life I could call and meet up with. I could try Paul, but I think he said he is away this weekend. I look up and see Sophie has come to sit beside me.

"So, Dave, a few of us have decided we don't feel like leaving yet and there is still wine left over on some of the tables, so we're going to stay a bit longer and keep playing some games. You in?"

The old me would have loved to be left in solitude, but again, what am I leaving for? There is a good chance Jenn is at the townhouse packing. I have no interest in that. So, I say I will stay. There are about twelve people staying back, and we all shift to one side of the hall and cluster the chairs together. We hastily grab all the leftover desserts and wine before the staff can clear them and decide to play another version of Pictionary. When I look around at who has stayed, it looks like the more junior staff or at the least, the ones who like to have a good time. It's a mix of the Marketing and Communications and Events teams and some other admin staff I haven't met yet. The mood is much lighter now. You can feel that Christmas is only a week away, and I find myself loosening up a bit and feel comfortable enough to join in the fun. This time it looks like I am on Sophie and Celeste's team. After a few rounds, it's now my turn to stand up to draw. I pull a card from the hat: Magic Carpet Ride. *No problem.* I'm pretty good at drawing and quickly draw a rectangle with an s-curve in the middle for depth, tassels on all four corners, and some Indian style design work. I draw some clouds and the sun in the background and some extra lines indicating motion.

Nothing.

Okay. I go the Disney route and draw an Aladdin-type figure on it quickly, as I'm running out of time. When I start working on the genie, I hear a faint question: "Magic Carpet?"

I start cranking my arm in a circle to indicate to keep going. "Magic Carpet . . . Ride?"

I turn and see that it's Celeste. She is smiling brightly. She looks at me with such intention, and I'm dazzled by her eyes, her smile. Everything about her is light and bright. There's brilliance but also a warmth, a comfort. It feels like everything stops for a moment, and I don't know how long we stare at each other. I feel a shift inside that I can't explain, and I don't know what to do with these emotions. Then someone walks up, grabs the marker from me, and I sit down next to Celeste. I want to be close to her. We spend the rest of the afternoon playing and drinking until it's time for everyone to go. I leave the yacht club and head home. Even though it's pouring rain, I feel sunshine somewhere.

CHAPTER 12 – CELESTE

We pack up and Sophie and I load her car with everything we brought from work for the party, then head back to the hospital to drop it all off. I stare out the window while she drives through the insane rainy Friday afternoon traffic, navigating through Kits to get us to the hospital. I am feeling something inside, but I don't want to name it because it feels like hope, and I really don't want to hope for anything these days. My hopes have been stepped on and squashed for so many years that it's a feeling I don't want to entertain anymore. That, or I feel scared to allow it to surface. If I'm being honest, I felt a moment happen between Dave and me. He was drawing a terrible sketch that made no sense and looked like chicken scribble and yet somehow, I guessed correctly. He turned his head, and his green eyes captivated me. It was like a sizzle of electricity passed between us, a cord of connection forming. I would normally pass off the look, but then he came and sat beside me, and when he walked over, it was like there was never another option, like he was only ever going to sit beside me. Through the rest of the games, it kept happening. It felt like it was just the two of us there playing and looking at each other, with everyone else as background characters.

And that is why I have to stop thinking it means anything. He was probably just happy to have made some friends, and maybe that is him just being friendly. My confidence isn't in a good enough place yet to hope that what that felt like could really be like what it felt like.

I am still lost in thought when we park, then keep dropping things as we try to carry all the overloaded boxes with Christmas decorations, supplies, and games back into the office. Suddenly I get a poke in the ribs.

"So . . ." Sophie says, giving me a side-eye.

I give her a side-eye back. "What?"

"Oh, you know," she says with a sly grin.

"I have no idea what you're talking about." Yes, I know what she is referring to. Maybe she witnessed what I think I also just witnessed. But I don't let myself go there. I can't.

"Oh stop it! I know you. You were so excited for today's Christmas party, but you got bummed when you sat at a different table. Then you conveniently decided to take all the photos, and when he said he would stay back and play with the rest of us at the end, your head almost exploded with glee. You're welcome by the way." She is laughing at me.

"Whatever could you mean?"

"Really, after waiting and planning every detail of this afternoon so that you could have a chance to talk with Dave, and then you have that 'moment.'" Sophie puts her fingers up in quotation marks.

We are now heading down the elevator and I just have to ask: "What do you mean, 'moment'?" I smirk at her. She knows me so well.

"Okay, finally! She admits it! You know what happened and I know it happened, but don't worry, I don't think anyone else saw it but me."

"Can you elaborate on what you mean exactly when you say 'moment'?" I don't want to provide any of my wishful thinking here and truly want to hear what she thinks she saw, because then maybe, just maybe, it wasn't made up in my mind, entangled in all my hopes and dreams.

"That moment when you solved his drawing and he turned around and you two just looked at each other. I could feel the heat of that stare and it was almost like no one else was there, but I was there, I saw it, it happened, and luckily, I don't think anyone else tuned into it or it would have just been awkward for everyone." She laughs. "But don't act like that didn't happen. You know it did."

We exit the elevator and open the office back doors and start dumping everything on the counter in the photocopy room to be put away on Monday. We turn around to head back to our vehicles.

"Celeste, this isn't in your head, girl. There is something there, and I'm just looking forward to watching how it unfolds." She gives me a big warm hug.

"What could unfold? He is probably just making friends. Maybe that's how he makes friends." I feel the lie on my tongue but really don't want to let myself hope that it could be what I think it is and that she also witnessed. That maybe, just maybe, we had a connection.

It's the last week of work before Christmas break and everyone was in a cheerful mood around the office. No events and fewer meetings. Preparing for the new year. Most nonprofits have a cycle of March to March, but the yearly cycle always brings in last-minute gifts from people who still want a tax break for this tax year.

Each day rolled into the next, and I only saw Dave once. I decided to avoid him, if possible, allowing me to live in my thoughts instead of testing out what may or may not have existed at the Christmas party. I wanted to head into the holidays with a glimmer of hope in my heart.

Thursday was the only day I spotted him. I was leaving the kitchen, and it looked like he was heading toward it. I saw him first down the hall of cubicles as he walked toward me. My stomach dipped, and I held my breath. As we passed each other, instead of saying hello like a normal person, I just stared at his lips. I didn't even make eye contact. It's possible he said hi, but I was in my head and didn't hear anything. Once I passed by him, I inhaled again, his lingering scent still with me as I headed toward my office.

It was another missed opportunity to show him that I was bright, talkative, and interested, yet every time I was in his presence, I clammed up and went mute. Or I stared at him. I must have looked like such a chump. Well, at least if he'd had any interest in me, I squashed it right out of him. Yep, it was for the best.

So, avoiding Dave felt like the best option so I didn't get confirmation that I had, indeed, made up that connection I thought we'd had. This way, I could live in my made-up dream world a little longer. Even though my heart rate sped up whenever I saw him and I felt such an intense pull toward him, I had to rein in my active mind.

Christmas this year is a different one—a good different one. Unlike previous "family" holidays where I had been left behind, this year I am included. My family history is a bit complicated. Over the years I have pulled away, mostly because I have never felt welcome. Since the divorce and the two families blended, I feel like I don't belong. It's like I am an honorary member who is asked to attend all the big events but who doesn't get the same courtesy of daily interest. It's like I check a box that I technically am a part of this family, but behind closed doors, they really can't care less if I am around.

So, most of my Christmases the last ten years have been spent with Mike and his family. This will be the first one in a long time when I am single and spending it with mine. It's pretty wild, really, that it was only a year ago that I wrote that list on my way to his parents' place. Who knew what could happen in a year's time? It is the list that changed everything for me. It made me finally decide that I could ask for more. That I could be with someone who deserved me.

It feels refreshing that Christmas this year looks nothing like the ones before, and it's amazing that my dad and stepmother have decided to take my brother, two stepbrothers, and me to Cancun over the holiday. So really, it's a perfect place to switch things up. To help me forget that I am starting from scratch.

We leave first thing in the morning a few days before Christmas. Maybe I can be someone else for a week. Someone who isn't insecure. I am tired of feeling pathetic. I am looking forward to finding that brave, confident woman who loves life. I know she's in there somewhere.

I looked out the front window of my dad's living room at my old high school sitting in the valley below, like a tribute to some of the best years of my life. A place that nurtured my adolescence. Back then we had just combined our families, and the people I met at high school became my everything. Home life had disintegrated, and friends became my family for five happy years. They distracted me from a home that didn't want me and helped my confidence grow. I became so sure of who I was, seen for my positive attitude, hard work, and kind offerings. These were the years that helped build my attitude that anything was possible. It's why I felt invincible and headed to the big city to try it all on. My friends and I were so optimistic about everything and everyone. I had secured good grades to make sure I could get into university. I was pursuing psychology because I had always loved giving advice to people and hoped one day to be a therapist.

I left the Okanagan so full of life, ready to take on any obstacle. I was up to trying anything. So, besides living in a new city on my own, with two new roommates, a new job, and navigating university courses, I decided to also try out drama courses. I took classes at the downtown campus, met drama friends, hung out on Commercial Drive, and eventually signed up for specialized classes. I ended up getting an agent and headshots and had a blast. I remember feeling fearless. I only lived in possibilities, never doubt.

Looking back, I realize how brave I had to be to put myself out in the world like that. To try something brand new at twenty-one and not waver at the intensity of this industry. To believe I belonged. And I did, for a bit. I got a role in the *Vagina Monologues*, reliving an experience of giving birth, and because I was last on stage, I had ample time for my nerves to ramp up and threw up backstage just before I went on, but I nailed the part and felt proud of myself. I also knew acting wasn't for me and I commend anyone who pursues this form of abuse because it is not for the faint of heart. That girl was maybe a little naive, but she was bold enough to follow her heart and take on anything she set her mind to.

The week at the resort flies by. I've found that an all-inclusive will do that, as one day blends into another. And before I know it, I'm on my way home feeling sun-kissed and relaxed, wishing it could be my everyday. This trip was a good way for me to start new traditions when it comes to Christmas. I appreciate that my dad and stepmom decided to treat us to something so unexpected, maybe an opportunity for us all to bond. We are all grown adults now, so spending time together lands differently and sitting around and drinking fits the bill at this stage of all our lives.

When we get back into town, it's time to spend a delayed Christmas with my mom in the Okanagan. Spending time with Mom has always been when I decompress. It's almost like I get too relaxed and all I do is sleep. I remember one afternoon when my stepdad used a sledgehammer to knock down the adjoining wall between the living room and the kitchen, and I was still able to nap! I guess that just means when I am in my mom's company, I have all my walls down and truly feel like I can be myself, that I can even sleep through power blows next to my head.

I've been feeling more sure of myself of late. The trip helped, with time on my own, sunshine, sand, and cocktails. I didn't even think about my current reality: single, no prospects in sight, and broke, but somehow, I didn't feel heavy.

I had time to remember who I was before Mike and also to realize that he doesn't take up any real estate in my heart or mind anymore. He did leave a hole where my self-esteem should be, but I have been feeling like I am coming up to the surface more and more. I'm feeling more optimistic and stronger for taking on the future.

I am sitting on the couch with my mom and we are both reading. I'm reading *The Notebook* for the twentieth time, and Mom is reading the autobiography of David Horowitz instead of her usual historical fiction. We're curled up knee to knee in our pj's. My mom wants to know how I'm doing. She was with me throughout my relationship with Mike and is aware of how broken I became over the years.

"What do you mean you are meeting people online?" She seems a little horrified because this is so far from her comfort zone. "How do you know these are really good men or anyone you would want to spend time with?"

"This is the new world, Mom. Meeting men in person is almost impossible. I can't only go to bars and try to figure out if they are decent while trying to carry on a conversation with music blasting."

"There has to be other ways."

"Here, I will show you the men I have been linked with." I open my computer and show her my matches. "I am hopeful I can meet someone on here. All these guys are looking to get married and be serious, so at least we have that in common."

"Okay, let me look." She squints her eyes and zooms in. "Who is this Pablo?"

He's a new match, and we both proceed to read his profile. Pablo actually seems promising and is quite cute too. "He looks like he could be great. We have lots of similar interests, and if we match, then it means the system has already told us we are compatible." I point to where he also likes snowboarding and rainy days. I decide to send him a message to see if we can connect when I'm back in the city. Time is of the essence.

"There must be another way to meet someone," my mom repeats.

I relent and decide to test faith and tell her about Dave. I don't want to because I don't want to jinx anything, and I truly feel like the more people I discuss him with, the more likely it will not happen. It will only lead to letting down more people when I tell them he isn't interested. But against my inner turmoil, I tell her about every interaction I have had with him since he started at the office. There isn't much to go on, but maybe her opinion on it won't be so bad.

"Do you have any photos of him?"

"Actually, I do. I was in charge of taking the photos at the Christmas party, but with all that free rein, I still only managed one terrible photo that is the top of his head."

I show my mom the overview shot of the table where he sat and curse myself for not getting a good photo of him looking all dapper at the Christmas party. I could have been staring at that picture every day instead of at the top of his head. But I remember why I never pointed the lens at him. I was so worried about how obvious I would be, so instead, I have photos of every other person and only a partial shot of him. I mean, at least he does have a great head of hair, hair that looks like it needs my fingers to loosen its curls.

My mom catches me lost in thought and clues into how bad I have it for Dave. "Okay, you said he likes to bake, so why don't you bake him something?"

"You know I'm not a baker. But I guess I could try and bake something for the office and maybe I could get his attention that way."

Mom smiles. "Well, that is a start."

Besides the fact that I can't bake, she does have a good point, and this could be a way to talk to him again, even if the voice in the back of my head is reminding me that I am trying to avoid him, not looking for ways to keep up my delusions. But my mom is giving me hope again. She is all in favor of the simplicity of meeting someone in person and not online. Of course, this is in line with what my gut has been telling me from the first moment I laid eyes on him.

So, the following day we come up with a plan. My mom has the best Nanaimo Bar recipe around, and she takes me out to shop for every single ingredient I'll need, even the baking pan. She then neatly writes out the instructions for me to ensure I can't go wrong.

When I leave the following day to head back to the city, she tells me, "I really feel like this Dave from work could be the real deal, Celeste, and I hope you call me soon with news that you and Dave are going out on a date and not you and Pablo."

I give her a big kiss and hug and then get in my car to start the five-hour drive to my stale, smelly, internet-free apartment back in the city, but this time armed with baking supplies to hopefully impress a man.

This holiday has been a bit of a turning point for me. I think getting out of the city and out of my normal routine was just what I needed. I feel a little bolder. I was reminded of who I am. Someone who likes to take chances and bets on herself. I am her, and I am ready to start trying again.

I have one day to prepare the Nanaimo Bars and package them up and bring them with me to work tomorrow. I also carefully plan my outfit so that if I get the opportunity to chat with Dave about my incredibly delicious treat, maybe he will get the idea that I am the snack.

New Year's Eve falls on a Thursday, which means the office is only open on Tuesday, Wednesday, and a half-day on Thursday, which makes for a pretty dead office. Most people take these as extra vacation days but usually the newbies and those with few vacation days left show up, enjoying the slow pace of an office half full.

Office culture has people bringing in treats all the time. They are shared with everyone. The protocol when you bring in treats involves sending out a companywide email to let everyone know. I craft a simple but tantalizing email to make sure anyone in the office knows there are delicious Nanaimo Bars in the kitchen and to please help themselves.

I press send and then the out-of-office emails start generating and Dave's is one of them. I totally thought he would be working because he's new and I didn't think he would take these days off, but nope,

FAST TRACK TO FOREVER

right there in black and white it says he won't be back to work until next week. Well shit, it's not like I can go retrieve my bars and hope they keep for another week. And I can't afford to make them all over again, not to mention it would look strange if I brought in the same treat twice within a matter of days.

How annoying! I slam my head down on the keyboard, defeated. Sophie stops by my office because she knows me so well and wonders why I brought a dessert into the office on a random workday. She is very aware I don't bake. She leans against my desk with her arms across her chest, then sighs.

I hang my head. "Don't look at me like that. I was just being nice."

Sophie chuckles. "Sure. Nothing to do with enticing Dave then. Ha! It's okay, just more for me."

"Yeah, but I keep doing this, wondering and hoping . . ."

And right when I am whining about what a waste of time this is, I hear the ping of a new email.

```
From: dpenni@foundation.com
To: cchild@foundation.com
Subject: Nanaimo Bars in the kitchen

Nanaimo Bars? Great, the one day I'm not there . . .
```

It's from Dave.

I proceed to stare at the screen. Why did he email me? Probably just being friendly.

With a huge smile, Sophie says, "Well, you need to reply."

"What would I even say? Maybe he is just being nice? I mean, he is new here and could be just trying to make friends."

But even as I say this, I am really hoping he emailed because it's me. My heart is pounding, and I feel like an excited sixteen-year-old when her first crush says hi in the school hallway. Seriously, my voice is caught in my throat, and I feel tingles all over. Tingles that are spreading through my body and making me feel full of hope and yearning. *It's just an email, Celeste.* It's so like me, my head spinning in circles. Being a hopeless romantic means that my thoughts can run many stories in my mind and sometimes I lose track of what's real. I lose touch with what's really happening and what I hope is happening. My intuition tells me Dave could be interested, but my brain tells me I am being foolish.

I have always believed in love stories that last forever. And then real life happened, and over the years with Mike, my love story just got more holes in it and my romantic heart became tarnished, and now I question everything. Which brings me back to the current moment. *How can I doubt myself so much I don't even know what to email back?*

Sophie elbows me in the ribs. "Earth to Celeste!"

"Okay, okay, what the heck do I say then? I need to be casual and not as eager as I feel." I put my face in my hands and take a few deep breaths.

"Something simple. Let's see what he has in him."

```
From: cchild@foundation.com
To: dpenni@foundation.com
Subject: re Nanaimo Bars in the kitchen

Hi Dave,

I guess it is your loss and now there is more for
me to eat.
Merry Christmas, by the way.

Kindly, Celeste
```

I press send. Okay, that was tame enough. It makes me sound aloof and not desperate. *Seriously, why do I feel so desperate inside?* It's from old wounds of that needy girl who only wanted to be seen and loved.

I am so tired of my upbringing making an impact on my life. I have already been to therapy. I know and understand why my dad made the decisions he did and the fact they had nothing to do with me, and yet I sit here not valuing what I bring to the table. When will I start believing in the person I know I am?

I look up at Sophie who is sitting on my desk. "Okay, I am about to combust. Let's go get a coffee, otherwise I will just sit here and stare at my screen, willing a reply. I didn't even ask him a question. Why didn't I ask a question and give him a reason to respond?"

I immediately feel stupid for not taking the opportunity to keep the conversation going. Seriously, I'm done playing small. It's time for me to ask for what I want, and the truth is, I want to see if there is a spark here with Dave. Even if he is just looking for friends, it's time for me to know either way.

I start standing up when my eyes catch an email landing in my inbox. I hold my breath, because it's a reply from Dave. I let out the breath and drop back down in my chair.

From: dpenni@foundation.com
To: cchild@foundation.com
Subject: re re Nanaimo Bars in the kitchen

Shame. I would have loved to try one of your bars. How was your Christmas? Mine was pretty low key. I spent it with my parents on the island.

Dave

A huge grin spreads over my face. He's talking to me. He replied, and right away might I add, and he has opened the conversation for us to keep chatting. This feels good, like maybe he is emailing because it *is* me. Maybe he felt that connection at the Christmas party too, and he is looking for an opening. *Okay, okay, chill Celeste, it's just an email.*

Sophie sees my face, reads the email over my shoulder, and smiles. "Come get me when you are ready to grab that coffee." She slips out of my office, leaving me bouncing in my chair.

```
From: cchild@foundation.com
To: dpenni@foundation.com
Subject: re re re Nanaimo Bars in the kitchen

Dear Dave,

Christmas on the island sounds lovely. Is that where
you are from?

I actually had a pretty great Christmas and spent it
in Cancun. Not normal for me, but my parents treated
us kids to a trip there over the break.

What are your plans for New Year's?

Sincerely, Celeste
```

I know it's bold of me to ask about New Year's, but I just had to give it a shot. What if he is in the city and is looking for something to do and I could be that something? I decided to reply with "sincerely" as my way of saying that I meant our exchange, that it mattered, but still sounded professional.

His response is almost immediate. He must be sitting at his computer, which makes me wonder if he is as up-front as I usually am. No point playing games.

From: dpenni@foundation.com
To: cchild@foundation.com
Subject: re re re re Nanaimo Bars in the kitchen

Wow. Cancun sounds a lot better than where I am. Sitting here with my parents and my dog sounds boring compared to where you got to go. Never been to Mexico. Maybe one day.

New Year's? I will also be spending it here with my parents, which sounds pretty depressing now that I mention it. Two weeks with my elderly parents sounded a lot more fun in my head. Do you have big plans? Staying in or going out? I may come back home early.

Dave

Oh my God! Did he seriously just imply he would like to get together? Am I reading this right?! I am dying inside and let out a little shriek. Sophie comes running in. "Okay, now what?"

I show her the email. "Please tell me this is a good sign? He is interested, right? I am so out of practice, I have *no idea* what flirting looks like anymore."

Sophie is totally laughing now. She hasn't dated in a while either, and at six feet, she has a strict policy of not dating anyone shorter than she is, so her pickings are slim. Sometimes I wonder if it's a bit of a defense mechanism. She is a bombshell: tall, slender, and confident, and she totally intends not to settle for anything less than what she deserves.

"Respond with something flirty. He opened the door; he is *definitely* interested."

My mouth drops open. "You really think he could be interested? Just from that one statement?" I feel like she is right, but I just don't know how to trust myself anymore.

Come to think of it, I think I lost my intuition ten years ago, the minute I moved to Vancouver. That's when I slowly lost my light, my optimism, my positivity, and certainly the trust in my intuition. Mike chipped away at that bright, hopeful girl who left her small town to find bigger things in the city.

Once you feel like all you do is make bad decisions, you can't help but think that maybe you have lost your inner compass. Which brings me back to what to reply. I feel myself deflate a little and remember I need to be realistic. So, I respond simply.

```
From: cchild@foundation.com
To: dpenni@foundation.com
Subject: re re re re re Nanaimo Bars in the kitchen

Hi Dave,
No big plans, just probably hanging out with some
girlfriends or by myself with a large jar of pickles.
Have a good rest of your day,

Celeste
```

I grab my coat and head out with Sophie to get our coffee. Instead of skipping while we cross the hallways of the hospital, feeling excited by our exchange, I actually feel weary. I felt so good there for a minute, until my mind caught up and reminded me to be logical. So, I had replied with a lame response and closed off the conversation.

Who am I to think this could be something, that he could want a relationship? I mean, the feelings I have when I look at him and when I am near him are probably all made up in my mind. It's probably just my active imagination, and I really don't feel like losing my optimism, so it's probably easier to stop.

Sophie doesn't push me when I get lost in thoughts. It's like she always knows I need time to process these situations.

I think back to Dave at the Christmas party in his seafoam-green shirt and wonder what he looks like with it off. I think about what it would feel like to have his hands on me and if I would like it. Whenever I think of Dave, a buzz goes through my body and I wonder if it is attraction, maybe even chemistry. But if any of my previous sexual interactions are any indication, I don't always have the best radar.

I drift back to memories of how I lost my virginity. Again, I believed it would be something so special, so magical, and yet it turned out to be a shrug of the shoulders by both of us. Like a why-not, I-guess-we-are-both-here kind of moment. It had been my senior year in high school, and to be honest, I was surprised I hadn't slept with any of my previous boyfriends. I'm sure they were interested, but it was something I never felt like doing, so they never pushed. I even had one boyfriend sneak into my bedroom at night, yet we never went further than the usual touching.

Every year after the last exam, a group of us would drive to our friend's property on Arrow Lake where we would spend a few days camping and releasing the stress from exams. It was the absolute best. Some days there were over fifty of us, and some days twenty, but every day had us all camping and hanging out around a big bonfire, drinking and smoking weed. We actually did this year-round too, but knowing we would all be together in such a big group for a few days helped us get through exams.

My senior year I was sharing a tent with my boyfriend, Devon. On the second night, Devon was standing behind me with his arms around me, and we were just staring into the bonfire, and I reached behind him and put my hands in his back pockets to feel closer to him. There was a condom in his pocket. I remember thinking it was as good of time as any, and I guess I saw the opportunity. I turned around, looked up at him and said, "Let's do it." So, my first time was quick, on an air mattress, in a tent surrounded by dozens of people. We fumbled around and did it like only two inexperienced teenagers can, only to realize afterward that the condom broke.

I panicked. I ran to Dallas's tent, because who else was going to help me solve this problem? I told her the whole story, crying my way through it, and I was so focused on myself that I didn't realize everyone could hear me.

The next morning, I took a "morning after" pill, was sick for three days, and never really spent much time with my "boyfriend" after that. It's kind of pathetic, going through a situation like that together, yet not even leaning on him or having him help or even wanting to talk to him about what I was going through. Of course, this was the time of landline telephones, so my whole family would have heard me if I discussed it with Devon on the phone. So, I handled it on my own with the support of my friend Sam who had been my ride back into town and to the clinic. Thankfully, everything ended up being okay, although not a good first experience with intimacy because it was more traumatizing than nourishing. I'm sure I'm not alone in having a first-time horror story.

It's just like me to always romanticize these situations, like I lived in *Beverly Hills, 90210*, and Luke Perry was going to whisk me away on his motorbike and make my first time feel as special as it's supposed to, like the feeling of being worshipped and taken care of. But fairy tales have only ever been experienced in my imagination.

Sophie and I arrive at Starbucks and order our Americanos. She is such a good friend; she doesn't even press me when she sees my range of emotions. She gives me space to process my own self-doubt.

I return to my office and wonder if Dave responded again, but nope, nothing there. Because why would he respond? He was probably just being friendly and really likes baked goods.

CHAPTER 13 – DAVE

I visited my parents for Christmas in BC while I was still living in Ontario, and once in the summer. Those two trips were the main reason I moved here. Originally, I was planning on moving to Victoria, but my mum thought it would be too much of a change from living in Toronto. Truth is, I don't really like living in big cities. I live in them because that's where all the jobs are. I'd much rather live in a small town.

Going to my parents' house was such a joy. I would hire a pet taxi for me and Tibby and then walk onto the ferry. The instant I got on the ferry, I'd relax. As it chugged out of Horseshoe Bay, passing Bowen Island and entering the open water of the Georgia Straight, I would breathe deeply, inhaling the salt air with a hint of sweet cedar. Because of Tibby, we weren't allowed on the upper deck, but there was no way we were going to spend hours in that makeshift bus stop they had for pets on the cargo level, so I would let Tibby off lead, and we would play hide-and-seek among the cars. At Christmas time, there were probably well over three hundred cars and trucks on board. I would run up and down the aisles between them, dodging in between any spaces I could find. It was Tibby's favorite game, and she would jump and pounce when she finally found me. It was a two-hour trip, and when she got tired, she would lie down on the lower car deck and feel the vibration and warmth from the engines below. My dad would be waiting on the other end in Nanaimo to take us home. The drive, once we left the ferry terminal, was probably one of the most peaceful drives one can imagine. Driving through small coastal towns, watching locals fish or dig for clams or, if you're lucky, catch a log barge dumping its cargo into the strait.

My parents' house was fully decorated for Christmas. The tree was in the front window facing the sea and had the same decorations it's had since I was a child. And on every tabletop and shelf were the same ornaments and knickknacks they had accumulated over their forty-five years of Christmases together. There were little trinkets on every surface. Snowmen, angels, reindeer, and Santas were sprinkled around the house. There were old cardboard spheres with silver glitter, cotton beards, and felt Santa hats from the seventies, as well as new ceramic Father Christmases from their recent travels to Germany. Both the placement and order of the decorations throughout the house were the same as previous years, and this brought me even further peace. The fire was burning, and mincemeat pies were cooling on top of the oven.

Within five minutes, I unpacked, Tibby was out playing in the yard with my parents' fat lab, Rosie, and I had an Old Speckled Hen in my hand. It was now officially Christmas.

"Place looks great, Mum. What's for dinner?"

"Shepherd's Pie. But I have one more batch of mince pies to finish before I can put it in the oven, so it will be another hour or so."

"Another beer, Dave?"

"Sure, thanks, Dad." The first one always goes down so fast.

"Any update on the townhouse?" asked Dad.

"Yep. It's pretty much a done deal, just waiting on their inspector to get back to us, and I should be out of there at the end of the month."

"Shame you have to go back and deal with all that at Christmas time. You'd think they could wait," said Mum.

"I don't care. I'm just happy that this is over and I'll be out of there soon. And I won't have to pay January's mortgage payment now, so I can use that for the rent deposit."

"You found a new apartment?" asked Dad.

"Yeah, it was pretty easy. I was walking past my old building last week and my landlord was out front doing some yard work. I asked if he had any units available and he said there would be one available once he finished the work on it. I said I would paint it for him if he let me have it for January, and he was fine with that."

"So Jenn was okay with the final price, then?" asked Dad.

"Not really, but then she was never really happy with anything. Again, I'm just glad this is almost over. This whole thing has been a fiasco."

"Oh well, lesson learned," said Dad. To be fair, I don't think he was really listening.

I think after Deirdre left, I became desperate. We talked about having children, and Deirdre was always tentative about the subject, once even saying that maybe we could adopt one day but never really engaging about it further. I didn't even ask why she wanted to adopt. I knew years before our relationship ended that she didn't want to have kids. She told me, in her own way, that she didn't, but I didn't want to listen. I just thought she would change her mind if we stayed together.

Jenn was the final attempt. On our first date, she asked why my last relationship ended. Dating in your thirties is like that. The questions are blunt and to the point. Everyone knows there's no time to dilly-dally, so the hard questions come first. My response was simple. "My ex didn't want to have kids. Do you want to have children?"

"Someday," Jenn replied. I didn't know until about eight months later that someday meant after her amateur rowing career was over, which she estimated was about seven years away. At least this time I made a quick run for the exit, but I knew from the beginning that it wasn't going to work, and I hadn't listened to myself. Again. So now, here I am, thirty-seven and single, with very little prospect for having a family.

"Yeah, I know, Dad. But it's not that easy nowadays. Things are more complicated." I don't know why they're more complicated. I think people make things more complicated than they are. "By the time you and Mum were my age you had three kids between the ages of eight and thirteen. You and Mum came to Canada with three hundred dollars, and within five years, you had a family and bought your first home for about fifty grand. That doesn't happen anymore. I had to go to university for four years, then two more years. My first job paid me two thousand a month and more than half of that went to rent. I worked my way up the salary ladder so I could barely afford a loft townhouse in Vancouver for almost half a million dollars." Dad has already tuned me out, which is fine, because I didn't want to talk about this anyway.

I am an early riser, but I still wake up the next morning about thirty minutes after my mum. We always sit and have coffee together and talk about old times, especially at Christmas, remembering the one Christmas when family came over from England, or when I got that one special present, or that year when we had two to three feet of snow. My mum's always proud of the Christmases she puts together. The older I'd get, the more she'd open up about Dad and how absent he was when we were little. "Your dad was just as surprised to see what you got for Christmas as you were," she would say.

My mum did everything. It would begin in October when she would start making the mincemeat for the pies. Then, in November, she would call us into the kitchen to stir the pudding. "Close your eyes and make a wish." We didn't have much money growing up, and my mum had to say no to a lot of things during the year. Apart from birthdays and back to school, we didn't have the money for extra things like clothes or other necessities, and especially not sweets, but Christmas was different: shortbread, sugar cookies, chocolates, mince pies, cherry cheesecake, and trifle. All made from scratch, all made with love, and all while working twelve-hour shifts, four days a week. And the tree was always jammed with presents. Sure, half of them were socks, underwear, and sweaters, but there were still so many toys. And then there was Christmas dinner, and with the exception of the brussels sprouts, which were boiled to oblivion, Christmas dinner was perfect. She would smother the inside of a paper grocery bag with about half a pound of butter and place the turkey inside the bag and tie the end with string to roast for the day. Inside the turkey was about two pounds of Paxo stuffing. Coupled with roast potatoes, and those wretched sprouts, drowned in turkey gravy, it is a memory relived to this day.

But there's something very different about Christmas morning as an adult without children. It still has a feeling, but the feeling is more on the luxury of time. More time to sleep. Now, I found the joy of Christmas came more from the extended break from work rather than an experience of the season itself. It became more about having time off, and unless you were in essential services, or really needed the money, you were guaranteed three days off. I was in the nonprofit sector where most offices closed for the week, so I didn't have to go back to work usually until January third or fourth. It was more about being out of the office: shopping, meeting friends, going to the pub, getting drunk, and not having to worry about being hungover the next day. It was about seeing family and celebrating that with even more booze and food. Even the presents were booze and food. But after a time, that celebratory feeling can wane, and you look for something different.

On this Christmas morning while Mum, Dad, and I had our coffee, I could feel the absence. It was fun to talk about my childhood Christmases with them, but I wanted to make my own memories. I wanted to watch my children run down the stairs in their pajamas, to open their presents, and to see that delight in their little faces.

Then, Boxing Day was all about watching Premier League football all day long, drinking pint after pint while eating turkey sandwiches and mince pies. But that feeling from Christmas morning returned, and my thoughts turned to heading home. I was supposed to stay at my parents' place until the new year, but the thought of spending another week there was starting to become unpalatable. The first few days were great, but after Christmas Day, the trip was devolving into a bit of a boozer. My thoughts were of going back, and in that moment, I decided I should check my email. I made a habit of checking, but not answering any emails over the holidays, filtering out any interoffice stuff that wouldn't be relevant when I got back so I would know what to focus on. I flagged a few things that would need looking at, but most were staff announcements about food. Constant notifications of chocolates or gingerbread, some kind of candy in the kitchen, with the corresponding "help yourself" immediately following. Thank God I wasn't there. I would gobble all that shit up. Then I saw an email from Celeste. Just seeing her name took me back to the Christmas party and the way she looked at me, and that feeling of light inside returned. Celeste's was the only email I decided to answer. We chatted back and forth a little. I decided to ask her about New Year's and what she was doing, and she mentioned something about pickles, which was confusing, but it appeared as if she didn't have any plans.

The next day, after coffee, breakfast, and a long walk with the dogs, my parents and I headed to the Crow and Gate, the best pub on Vancouver Island as far as I'm concerned, and the closest thing to an authentic country pub outside of Britain. I've never been in the summer, but it apparently has amazing gardens. However, we go for the rainy weather, cozy fireplace, dark wood floors, darts, and bar service instead of table service, which is much more efficient. We get a table right next to the fireplace. It's about three feet wide and two feet deep and warms you to your bones. We all order the ploughman's lunch and Dad and I get a pint of Smithwicks. I came here last year and was so looking forward to it, but now that I'm here, all I think about is going home. I think about moving into my new place, understanding my new job, and starting a new life. I think back to the Christmas party, to Celeste, how she moved across the room, how she made everyone feel. I think of her smile.

When we return to my parents' house, I tell them I'm going to return home early and start moving into my new apartment. I find Celeste on Facebook and her profile is public, so I scroll through her photos and find some from her thirtieth birthday party the previous year. She's six years younger. That works. I also find some photos of her on a beach in Mexico with some guy. It's pretty old, and he doesn't appear any time after that, and she said she didn't have any plans, so I decide to send her a message on Facebook to see if she's interested in getting together the weekend after New Year's when I'm back in Vancouver. I suggest a coffee. I thought I should be cautious, not only because of the recent blunder with Jenn, but if this went sideways and I still had to work closely with her, it could get awkward. Dating a coworker is not always the best idea, and frankly, it was making me a bit nervous.

But for whatever reason, I felt it was worth it. I try not to overthink these things.

It's been four days, and I haven't heard back from Celeste. It looks like she hasn't read the message. Did I misread things? How did I get that so wrong? I've had so much on my mind with the selling of the townhouse and the move, I would not be surprised if I misinterpreted things. Still, I expected at least a reply. Totally cool if you're not interested, but at least send a response. Why make it more awkward than it needs to be? Trying to communicate via texts and chats can lead to misinterpretations. I always prefer to talk in person, so you can read them better, watch body language. I'll see her in the office tomorrow and I'll get a better sense then. Maybe she's just waiting to do the same, to talk in person. I'm being way too optimistic. Women communicate just fine through text. I've pinned a lot of emotional hope on this, and I promised myself I wouldn't, so I slide back into my mental mantra. *Being on my own isn't a bad life, just a different life. Tibby and I will drive down the American West Coast, hike in the Sonora Desert. I'll do the coast-to-coast walk in England. Take that train from Barcelona to Mykonos.* I've run it all in my mind hundreds of times. It usually works, but now all those things just sound like filling empty time, and I can't suppress the disappointment I'm feeling. I had really hoped this might have been something. It felt right.

CHAPTER 14 – CELESTE

Well, that was an uneventful weekend and a pathetic New Year's. I watched a movie with my neighbor Nicole and was in bed before midnight. Yep, that's the wild life I live. Daydreaming of a life filled with love and adventure and trying to not let it be Dave's face that creeps into my mind. Dreaming we are both at a party, him looking at me across the room, then walking straight up to me right when the clock ticks down and giving me the most passionate kiss of my life. A kiss that makes promises and tells you your dreams might just come true after all. It was the best kind of daydreaming before I fell asleep.

I get ready for work that morning as I would any other morning. I pick my favorite dress, black to fit my mood, the one with the large shoulder pads because then it will give the look of a waist and it also hides the fact that I ate a lot over the last two weeks. I always wished I had one of those hourglass bodies so that when I gain some weight it will go to my hips or boobs, but not me: mine goes straight to the middle so everyone always knows when I eat that extra piece of cake. I pair the dress with my electric blue tights and my comfy black booties. At least this outfit makes me feel confident; I can walk and still feel tall and slender. When I get outside, I look up and see the clouds are high in the sky and there's no immediate rain in sight, which is strange for a Vancouver day in January. So, I decide to walk to work because driving my car and paying for parking is a luxury I don't have right now.

I grab my navy blue peacoat and red scarf and head to work. The streets are clear, and the temperature is brisk. That is one positive of winter in Vancouver: when it's not raining, the weather is decent. I arrive at work, head up the stairs, and peak into Sophie's office to say hello. She is already in and gives me a big smile. "Okay, girl, coffee in thirty minutes and you can catch me up on everything that went down for your big New Year's!"

I laugh. "Yeah, okay, because I already texted you, you know I did nothing. And you know that saying that how you bring in New Year's will determine the rest of the year? So, yeah, I guess you can say this year will be pretty uneventful." I roll my eyes and head over to my cubicle.

I hear Sophie's departing voice as I go: "No one says that, Celeste."

I load up my computer, put my coat away, and daydream a little about my Christmas break. It had been a good break, mostly because I feel like something shifted in me a bit. I feel more stable and grounded and glimpse a return to my old self, but I'm now a wiser, more independent version. I've come in a few minutes early so I can check my private email and social media. There is nothing out of the ordinary in my emails, just the usual spam and exercise motivation because, well, it is a new year. One is for a free kickboxing class tomorrow night. Maybe I'll ask if Dallas wants to go with me after work.

I open up my Instagram account and honestly, I don't care to scroll through everyone else's New Year's parties just to see how happy everyone looks. So, I open Facebook and see I have a new message. It's from Dave. With shaking hands, I open it.

Hi Celeste, I hope it's okay that I sent you a message here, as I know this is your personal account, but my request is personal so thought this was a better place to ask. Are you free this weekend by chance? I know you said you had plans for New Year's, but maybe would you like to grab a coffee earlier in the day?

Well, shit! I feel fireworks in my belly! Why would he send me a message here if he might not be interested? And he was in town? And I missed this and could have seen him on New Year's? My mind is reeling, and I can't believe I haven't seen this message until today. What do I say now? *Okay, be cool, be cool!*

Hi Dave, Happy New Year! First, I am sorry I am just seeing this message now. I don't have internet at home and couldn't check my Facebook until I got to work (don't tell anyone). I would totally like to get a coffee. Should we try for next weekend?

With nervous hands, I minimize the screen so that my colleagues who are just getting into work can't see that I have Facebook open, and just in time because my boss comes in to say hello and ask how my holidays were. I try to keep it short and to the point because I really need her to move along. I am dying to see if Dave has seen my message and replied. Then, my other boss walks in and starts the chitchat too. I am normally super chatty, always looking to make people feel good, but argh, not right now. So, I give short answers. After what feels like forever, which probably was only five minutes, they head into their respective offices and I load up Facebook again, and holy crap, there is a message from Dave.

117

Good morning, Well, that would explain why I didn't hear back from you, as I was wondering if maybe I had crossed a line or maybe you were seeing someone. Tomorrow night me and my friend are heading for a drink at the Three Lions Pub. Would you be interested in joining us?

Dave, I was planning on kickboxing, but a beer definitely sounds better. No boyfriend, by the way

Great! I would suggest a coffee today, but my day is crazy with meetings and catching up after the holidays, but maybe I will run into you. Talk soon

Okay, this is too much. I calmly but quickly walk myself over to Sophie's office and stand in the entry with a big silly grin on my face. I don't want Simon to catch on to my elated mood. This is not info he needs to have right now. So, I try to use my eyes to make her get up and follow me. She makes a face, furrows her brows, and then it's like a lightbulb turns on and she makes an "oh" with her mouth.

"Celeste, can you show me the presentation edits you made to the marketing deck for new vendors?" she says as she runs out of her office, and I lead her down the hall where no one can hear us. I practically scream in the quietest mouse voice I can muster and tell her about the messages.

Her eyes light up, she pushes my shoulder, and I stumble back a little. "Hey, what was that for?"

"Because, you twit, I told you he was interested. I saw the way he was looking at you at the Christmas party *and* the tone of his emails last week!"

"Okay, so what are we going to do now?"

"*We* are not going to do anything. I am going to go back to checking the huge number of emails I need to get through, but *you*, well, I think you should just keep being yourself." And as she leaves me, laughing, she yells, "Come grab me to get a coffee once you have calmed down. I think you still owe me one."

I stand leaning against the wall for a few more moments with a big grin on my face.

Okay, deep breath, Celeste. He just asked you to join his friend and him for a drink, it's not like he asked you to have his baby. And remember, you might not like him; you don't even know him. And you swore to yourself that this time you would only spend time with someone who meets your criteria. I remember the list I made, the very one that brought me the clarity I needed to break up with Mike. I can't abandon it now just because I want to jump his bones. No, I have to do this right. I have to keep my standards high.

At least I know he fulfills numbers one and two on the list: a great smile and beautiful white teeth. Wow, if those are numbers one and two, I might need to up my standards a little more. Gah, why do I feel like a schoolgirl just thinking of him? My mind goes to so many places it has no right to go. I am already picturing us married with two kids. It's time to rein in those horses. I take a deep breath and head back to my office.

Later that day I head into the kitchen to grab my lunch, put my day-old mac and cheese in the microwave, and run to the bathroom. As I'm walking back through the kitchen door, I hear a low voice just over my shoulder. "Wait a sec," Dave says, and my whole body shivers.

I slowly turn my head and give Dave a huge grin. He strides toward me with his purposeful walk and then he is standing one foot away from me. He is about half a foot taller than I am, and I am already tall. He stops and gives me the smallest little grin and I can feel myself getting excited. Oh, am I in trouble! One little bit of hope and I am off to the races.

"Hi, Dave, welcome back. Catching up on all your emails?"

"Hey, Celeste, yep, pretty much caught up." I like the sound of my name coming from his lips. *Am I drooling?* I think I am drooling. I wipe my mouth and quickly look at his lips. *Oh shit, how is it possible for a man to have lips like this? Top and bottom are both pouty and plump, but masculine. They look like the perfect color of dark pink, like pillows that I could sleep in for hours. I think I just heard my name.*

Oh wait, look up, he is looking at me. How long have I been staring?

"Celeste?"

"Oh, yes, hello, sorry, not sure where I just went there." And he gives me a smirk that tells me he didn't miss a beat of where I was staring.

He nods at the door. "Shall we go in?"

"Oh, yes, of course." I turn just as my cheeks start to go red and quickly make my way to the microwave to take out my lunch, which is already out because others are waiting.

I sit down with two other colleagues, both older employees who have worked here for a while. But out of the corner of my eye I can see Dave grab his lunch from the fridge and sit down at the same table. He opens up a brown bag to reveal a cheese and tomato sandwich, a container of neatly cut carrots sticks, and a huge green apple. Definitely healthier than mine. *Okay, I can do this. He is only two feet from me, but I can be normal. It's not like he asked me for drinks just a few hours ago. Let's see if I can be cool, because I don't want our colleagues catching on to whatever this is.*

I sit and eat my gross lunch and listen to Dave kindly chat with the others. He asks them about how long they have worked here, where they live in the city, and what parts they like best. I get lost in listening to Dave chat with them. He is very attentive and asks good questions.

My mind tunes in and out of their conversation while I eat my lunch.

Patricia looks at me. "Celeste lives close to you I think, right, Celeste? Don't you live in that area?"

I don't look up because if I do, I will lose my cool here. "I do. I live on 8th and Yew."

Dave turns his whole body in my direction. "No way, that's like two blocks from me. I wonder why we haven't crossed paths before." Again, I have lost my voice as I stare, so he continues on. "Do you drive or walk to work?"

I can manage this one. "I walk. I have a car, but I like the walk."

"Well, I am walking home today. Shall we walk together?"

This is actually happening. Dave is talking to *me* and asking to walk home with *me*. This is my life right now. From months of wondering whether he noticed me to now this. I feel like I am walking on cloud nine. I really hope it's not written all over my face, even though I'm sure I'm blushing.

I take a deep breath. The whole table is looking at me. I look Dave right in the eyes and say, "That would be nice. I mean we are going the same way anyway."

CHAPTER 15 – DAVE

Well, today turned out much better than expected. After half a week of thinking that Celeste had no interest, it turns out that she just can't afford the internet at home. This, and the nutritional dearth of her lunch, has me thinking there are quite a few financial constraints at home. But I found out that she's not with anyone and is having a drink with me and Paul after work tomorrow and said she would bring a friend. I've known Paul for years, and he's easy to talk to; and if things go well between Celeste and me, he'll pick up on it and find a reason to leave.

When I bump into her outside the kitchen, she gives me a shy smile. She's wearing another outfit that is burning my eyes: shocking blue tights, and the outfit is some kind of black inverted triangle space suit with padded shoulders. I shrug it off as Celeste takes her shambles of a lunch to a table with some people from gift processing or something. We chat over lunch and find out we live only two blocks from each other but have never bumped into one another, so I take advantage of this new knowledge and ask if she wants to walk home together after work.

At 4:29 p.m., I close down my computer and head upstairs to Celeste's office. I tap on her door, and she looks up with that smile again and everything stands still. She turns back to her computer, shutting it down, does a bit of organizing for the next day, and says a quick goodbye to her officemate before we leave. We don't say anything to each other, she just grabs her purse and coat and we head out, but not before I see the funniest smirk on Sophie's face as she watches us leave. We head down the stairs out of the hospital and head toward 10th Avenue. It looks like we both walk this route because we didn't even need to discuss it, like we have done it a number of times but never together. It's a beautiful afternoon with the sun close to setting. The drop in temperature has the air feeling crisp, which is a nice break from the rain.

"So," I say as we fall into stride with one another.

"So," she says, but it doesn't last long before we both jump into questions about one another.

"So how long have you worked at the Hospital Foundation?" I ask first.

"Well, I think I am coming up on five years now. I really love it there, especially because I can walk to work." She looks my way and gives me a little smile and then continues. "I started at the front reception as a coordinator and did a bunch of events too, then got the promotion to support my three directors. It's been a solid place to work. My first job out of university was in East Vancouver helping at-risk youth find employment, but after a few years I needed a change." She takes a breath and continues again. "It wasn't like I got burned out like everyone says happens, but it was watching these kids and some adults and the decisions they made. No matter how many good opportunities I found for them, they always found a way to sabotage it, found a way to quit even though they had kids at home to feed. I got my degree in psychology and wanted to help because I wanted to inspire them. To let them know they could live meaningful lives, but what I came to realize was that by the time they came to me for help, it was almost too late to turn anything around. They needed some kind of earlier intervention. Because it was like they had already been programmed to not believe they could have empowered lives. Mostly, it looks like they just needed to be loved and held when they were babies, and I don't think most of them had that. Okay, I am rambling . . ."

But the more she talks, the more I want to listen. She continues sharing about her experience in East Vancouver, which I find fascinating. I'm sure her sunny disposition was needed in that part of the city. She even volunteered at a youth prison. As Celeste shares this small part of her life, I can feel the empathy and kindness that's in her. I've waited my whole life for someone like this.

We walk in silence as we cross Granville and then I hear Celeste ask, "So what about you, Dave, have you always worked as a researcher?"

I smile. "Actually, I got my master's in library science."

Celeste turns and gives me the funniest look and says, "Sorry, what does that even mean?"

I laugh. "It means I intended to be a librarian, hence all the cardigans and tweed hats. They're compulsory." We both chuckle and I continue. "I actually started out as a librarian and got a really great job at InBev right after graduation. I did research and document delivery services for scientists all over the world, and I cataloged the research materials InBev was collecting. But they relocated the library to Belgium, so I was only there for a year or so. To this day, it was the best job I ever had. They gave us so much free beer. I originally wanted to be a university librarian, but I needed a second master's degree for that so I went to Acadia, but I couldn't do the student thing anymore and just snapped and quit the program. Then I found out about prospect research in the nonprofit sector and got an entry level job doing that. Turns out I was quite good at it, so I've been doing that and moving up in position ever since. Now, I'm getting more into campaign planning, database management, and reporting, which are pretty dry, but I still love the research part of the work."

"So, you have two degrees . . . how much are your student loans?"

"Well, three as far as the loans," I respond. "Even though I dropped out of my second English degree, I still have to pay for it. And, yeah, it's been crippling. I received a small inheritance from my grandmother, and I was able to pay off half of it, but I still have to make four-hundred-dollar monthly payments. It's the reason I could never afford a car."

"Same for me. When I started having to make those payments, well, let's just say the jobs I could get out of university did not pay nearly enough. It's been rough."

Sharing our stories makes me feel calm. I don't feel like I am trying to impress her. I can be open with her. We are just sharing who we are, and it feels easy. I can just be myself. Whenever she looks my way, I catch her soft brown eyes, she smiles, and my heart fills.

"I should probably mention that I recently broke up with my ex. We were together for a little over a year. We lived together, but she wasn't for me, nor I for her. Actually, the whole thing was pretty toxic at the end. I finally realized that I was the only one trying, and she basically wasn't a very nice person. At times I thought that this was the best I could get, but I realized it would be better to be on my own with Tibby than with someone who doesn't even like me." *Wow, I have never voiced that out loud. It felt good!*

"Oh, who is Tibby?"

"Tibby's my dog. She's a lab cross, almost five. She's probably the sweetest dog you'll ever meet. I take her to Kits Beach every day and the Endowment Lands on the weekends. She's helping me enjoy Vancouver so much. She's been everything to me for the last few years. It's been hard moving out here and starting over, but she's helped me through it. However, Tibby also has shit recall and likes to roll in goose poo. So, there is balance." This seems to get another big smile from Celeste. *Cool, looks like she likes dogs.*

"Well, I was in a long relationship that ended just under a year ago. It wasn't a healthy one, and I think I am still learning how to be with myself. I mean, I know I don't want to be with Mike. He wasn't healthy in a lot of ways, and he did a number on my self-esteem, which I am still looking to find somewhere. But I also feel the best I ever have. I feel hope, like I am finally heading in the right direction." She sighs and gives me a smile. "Does that make sense?"

"Yeah, I can relate."

Celeste then furrows her brow. "Okay, so you have a dog, you're tall, fit, have a great smile, and you have lived two blocks from me for almost three years and we have never run into each other? How is that possible? Because I know I would have noticed you." She is so honest and up-front, it's refreshing. It's like you always know where you stand, and she doesn't play games.

"Pretty sure I would have noticed you too."

I see her grin at this. "Maybe we just weren't supposed to meet yet," she says softly. "The thing is, I made a list a year ago of what I was looking for in a partner, and well, that very list is how I got brave enough to break up with my ex, because he was none of the things I was looking for. The list was almost my permission to leave him; it gave me the strength to see him through new eyes. I feel like this list is my road map; it's what will tell me if I have found the right person." She tucks her jacket closer around herself, almost like she wants to disappear.

"Well, Celeste, I think it's good to know what you want, and I know I don't know you that well, but from what I can tell, you deserve to have everything you want on that list." *I wonder how I can get hold of this list to see how I stack up and quickly fill any gaps, if needed.*

Before we know it, we've walked the whole way home; it felt like five minutes. We stop in front of the dry cleaners on the corner of Arbutus and Broadway, where I need to pick up some shirts. We turn to face each other and I ask her a question that I have on my mind. "So, why don't you have internet at home?"

She looks down and a bit sheepishly says, "I can't afford it. When my ex left, well, I don't have many funds for anything extra, and right now, internet is an extra."

I want to wrap my arms around her, she looks so vulnerable, and I want to make her smile again, but I don't know what to say. "I am looking forward to tomorrow night and drinks will be on me."

We stand there again, smiling at each other. It's like a magnet is pulling us closer and closer and just when I am wondering if trying to kiss her would be a good or bad idea, she puts her hand on my arm and turns to leave. "Well, thank you for the walk home, Dave. I really enjoyed talking with you."

I'm left standing there feeling like a schoolboy in love. Celeste is so gentle and has nothing but concern for others. I can't understand how someone could take such advantage and start to get a bit angry. Probably because the same thing has happened to me. I didn't start out so cynical, but when people take advantage of you over and over, you start to harden. But not Celeste. She still has a light in her, a tenderness that remains. I don't think I could play it cool if I tried.

CHAPTER 16 – CELESTE

I am reeling! Walking home with Dave was more than I could have ever hoped. It was so easy to talk to him. He didn't seem repelled by anything I shared and was intrigued to learn more about me. Could he really be interested in me? The more I get to know him, the more I like. There were moments when he just looked at me, like he saw me, like he thought maybe I was something special. I felt confident in his eyes, like being myself was always the plan.

I feel invigorated and am dying to share, so I call Dallas. I had already texted her to see if she could be my "wing woman" for a drink with Dave and his friend.

Dallas picks up immediately. "Okay, so tell me everything!" I've always been so thankful for her support. I proceed to tell her about our conversation, how he stopped and stared at me, and how everything had felt so effortless, so easy.

"He likes you!"

"Oh, come on, Dallas. We have had one conversation, maybe two if you count the one outside of the office before lunch. He could just be being friendly."

"Oh no, you don't get to downplay this. He asked you about relationships—that was interest. I can hardly wait to take a look myself tomorrow. You sure have built up the whole tall, dark, and handsome visual."

"But you have to act cool tomorrow. No crazy questions. And no telling pathetic stories about me."

"No promises. I've got to run, so text me tomorrow for the time and I'll see you there."

We hang up and I scream. This feels too much; he did seem interested. His gaze felt intense. Oh, how am I going to sleep tonight? Time to plan my outfit for tomorrow. *What will convey future wife material?*

I barely sleep and when I do, Dave's genuine smile fills my dreams.

I arrive at work the next day with an extra spring in my step. I'm bursting inside. I'm not sure how I will make it through the day with the anticipation of hanging out with Dave some more tonight.

I load up my computer and sign into the normal social media accounts with wishful thinking there will be a message from Dave, but alas, no. Early in the morning I go and get a coffee with Sophie and fill her in.

She is so excited for me. "Oh, he is interested, Celeste. Stop trying to act like he isn't. Trust me, I saw his face when you two left the office together yesterday. He only has eyes for you."

I inhale slowly and smile. "I just don't want to get my hopes up. We still barely know each other, and it's possible he is just looking for friends."

"That's true, or he could want to eat you up like the deliciousness that you are."

"Stop it. Don't get my head going or I won't be able to get any work done today. It's already a challenge."

"The more important question, though, is do you like what you're finding?"

"Without question, yes. The more I learn about him, the more intrigued I am. There is something when I am with him that is hard to articulate. It feels almost cosmic."

"Well, just make sure you don't compromise anything you're looking for."

I think back to the list. Might be time to go find that journal.

I return to my desk and to an email from Dave.

```
From: dpenni@foundation.com
To: cchild@foundation.com
Subject: Tonight

Good morning, Celeste, just wanted to let you know
that I am looking forward to tonight. I might not
see you at lunch because I have to run home and walk
Tibby. I don't want to worry about her this evening.
So, how about I see you at the bottom of the back
steps outside at 4:35 p.m.?

Dave
```

Oh my God! He's looking forward to tonight!

```
From: cchild@foundation.com
To: dpenni@foundation.com
Subject: re: Tonight

Dave, the day is going painfully slow. See you in a
few hours.

Celeste x
```

Maybe the "x" is a little forward of me, but I can't help it. I feel like we have a connection, and I am hoping he feels it too. For months I had waited for him to notice me, and I feel like he sees me now. I am seriously counting down the minutes and can hardly wait for tonight.

As soon as 4:30 p.m. arrives, I send a text to Dallas that we will be there by 5:00 and to get her ass in the car as she will be coming from North Vancouver and I know traffic in this city can be insane and I don't want it to be awkward with just me, Dave, and his friend. I head down the back stairs, open the back door to the parking lot, and there he is.

Tall, dark curly hair, and penetrating gaze, he is wearing a black trench coat over a white collared shirt, a navy-and-yellow striped tie, and black work slacks, and he looks like the definition of drinkable. Like seriously, I cannot stop staring, and it might be because he seems to be looking at me the same way, like he likes what he sees.

I walk up to him, and we are two feet apart just looking at each other, then he breaks me from my stupor before I can articulate words by saying, "Shall we, Celeste?" and sweeps his arms in the direction we will be walking in toward the pub.

We fall into step together and immediately pick up where we left off yesterday, like talking with one another is the most comfortable thing and we have been doing it for years.

"So, you seriously walked all the way home to take Tibby out on your lunch? Because the timing doesn't really add up when we only have an hour for our lunch. It takes us twenty minutes to get to our neighborhood."

He chuckles, almost like I caught him. "Well, I can be a very fast walker when I want to be. I made it home in fifteen minutes, then threw the ball for Tibby for twenty minutes, then got back to work in time to eat my lunch. Besides, I always work while I eat my lunch. I'm not one for chitchat in the lunchroom."

"Except for yesterday, you seemed very chatty," I add.

"Maybe I had incentive." He smirks.

I actually do agree that he is a very fast walker, and I have to double my steps every little while to keep up.

"So, what do you get up to at night when you don't have any internet, Celeste?" The way he says my name makes a spark ignite inside me and I want him to say it again and again, just so I can feel this feeling.

"Well, I still have cable, so I usually watch *Seinfeld* reruns and hang out with Max." He almost stumbles on the sidewalk and looks away. It isn't until we are waiting to cross the street at the next light that he quietly asks who Max is.

I laugh out loud, realizing what he must think. How had this not come up yesterday when we talked about his dog? Once we get onto Broadway, he positions himself to be closest to the street and we start walking again.

"Max is my cat." I notice an audible exhale from Dave before I continue. "When my ex came to pick up his things last summer, well, it was while I was at work, and when I got home that day, I knew he had planned to come by, but what I didn't know was that he was also planning to take our cat, the cat I had been living with for months. She always talked to me, and I still miss her." I take a breath and notice his fists are clenched. "It's okay, though. I was more upset that he took Lucy than I was over our breakup. Which speaks volumes, so I guess missing the cat over him was good confirmation that I was completely over him. But mad as hell that he took our cat. And then a few months ago someone from my floor hockey team said they needed to find a home for their cat Max, and I volunteered."

"Yeah, having a fur friend is the best. Floor hockey, eh? How long have you been playing?" He asks as he gently puts his hand on my lower back to guide me around a group of people.

"Just over a year, I think. A friend joined and she asked if I wanted to play too. There really wasn't any experience required, only attendance."

"Interesting."

"It's a lot of fun, and I love the women on my team."

We walk in step with each other as we continue along Broadway, chatting with ease. It feels like I have known Dave forever, and there are no pauses in our conversation. It is like we're both trying to learn as much as we can about each other.

"Dave, I have to ask, and I understand if you don't want to answer, but how old are you?"

"How old do you think I am?" He asks with a grin.

I elbow him in his ribs. "Well, I have a feeling you're a few years older, just not sure by how many."

"Six years older."

"What?" I stop on the spot. "Does that mean you know how old I am?" I smile up at him.

"Yeah, of course. Celeste, I am a researcher, and I always investigate possible drinking mates."

"That makes no sense, Dave."

He chuckles and wraps his fingers around my elbow, sending a tingle all the way up my spine and down to my toes. Then he grabs it a little more firmly and turns me so we start walking again. But his hand doesn't leave my arm, and that's all I can feel. His firm fingers gently guide us, and I never want to lose contact.

"Ha ha, caught me. Yes, I saw how old you were when I stalked you on Facebook."

"Stalked me? Well, what else did you find?"

"Too much, I'm afraid. I'll have to help you set up your privacy settings. But what I did find was intriguing."

I feel butterflies everywhere. He is intrigued by me! That's a good sign!

Before we know it, we have arrived at Three Lions Pub. Dave places his hand on the door, but instead of opening it, he turns to me and looks me right in the eyes. "Celeste, I hope you know that it was a really shitty move your ex made by taking your cat, and if I ever see him, I will break his nose."

I give him a grin. "Well, that does seem a little extreme, but thank you for agreeing it was a dick move." And with that, Dave opens the door, his other palm resting on my lower back.

We spot his friend Paul and Dave sits across from him, so I sit beside Dave on the bench seat. Paul seems nice enough, and I take a moment to text Dallas to ask where she is. I just hope that it's not her usual lateness since she knows I need her here to balance this out.

I am sitting close enough to Dave that I can smell him, and it does something to me that feels personal. It's like it was made for my pheromones, as if I can breathe it in deep and get lost in the ocean of his DNA. His friend keeps looking my way, and I hope I haven't been too obviously leaning and sniffing.

I pull myself back to reality and check out the menu. Dave and Paul are busy chatting about what beers they are getting.

Dave looks over at me with a slight smile. "What can I get you, Celeste?"

I am about to answer when the door opens and Dallas walks in. Perfect timing. She arrives at the table with her huge grin. The men stand and I introduce them. There are handshakes all around, then Dallas sits down across from me and with no subtleness whatsoever cups her hands around her mouth to whisper "HOT," and I kick her under the table because she is way too obvious. She is supposed to be making me look good!

We all order a beer and our food, and Dallas and I catch up a little while Dave and Paul chat. Dallas fills me in on her latest argument with her husband and keeps getting distracted by texting back and forth with him. It's typical. Together or apart, they can't get enough of picking at each other, at least lately.

Our food promptly arrives and the evening progresses with easy chitchat and getting to know each other, but I can't seem to get my attention off Dave and away from asking him questions about himself. I can't get to know him fast enough, and Dallas is distracted with her phone and has lost interest. Truth be told, I have Dave's attention. His thigh has been pressing against mine all night, and my whole body can't stop focusing on the place our bodies connect. It already feels like a live wire.

Paul appears to notice that the conversation keeps coming back to Dave and me. I am truly not doing this intentionally but can't help myself. Soon, Dallas says she has to go, drops some cash to cover her bill, and kisses me on the cheek. Right before she exits the door, she looks back at us and gives a very silly half smile to the whole table, basically implying what we are all feeling: She is a passenger in the Dave and Celeste show.

Within minutes, Paul has the same idea and gets up to pay his tab. Super polite, he offers me his hand. "Celeste, it has been great meeting you, but I think I'm an extra on a date here, so I will leave you two to it." He smiles and walks out the door.

I keep my head down, embarrassed, as I never like to make anyone uncomfortable and not welcome. And a date, really?

I look up and see Dave looking over at me with a smirk. "Maybe I should have just asked you out on a date instead of having my friend join us." Butterflies erupt in my stomach. I feel winded. He is interested! It's not just me; he feels this too. I stare back into the depths of his beautiful green eyes and give him a genuine smile.

"Official date or not, I am enjoying spending time with you, but I do feel bad that I didn't engage Paul very much, and that was rude of me."

"Ah, he's fine. We meet for beers all the time. He was distracting me from you, so I'm thankful he left."

I am reeling with happiness and allow myself to enjoy this minute. I had wondered about and imagined it for so long, and now I'm here, and Dave and I are engaged in getting to know one another. It feels so right and easy.

We carry on with conversation for a while, and with each minute, it seems like we inch closer and closer. We're sitting side by side in this noisy pub, and yet all I see is Dave.

I keep catching him staring at my mouth and then he leans closer and whispers in my ear, "I really want to kiss you right now."

Oh my God! Did he really just say that? Play it cool, Celeste. Deep breath. "Well, I would love to have you kiss me, but I don't think our first kiss should be sitting here in a bar."

He slowly looks around and observes the people we have totally been tuning out, then nods. "Yeah, good point."

Dave is interested, he wants to kiss me, and now it's all I can think about and I can't stop staring at his lips. I have been wanting to test them out for a while now. He takes a drink of his pint as I stare at his plump lower lip carefully straddling the glass, at his Adam's apple bobbing while he swallows. All I feel is heat in my core and my rational mind is gone—I am jealous of a glass.

Who am I kidding? Do I really care if our first kiss happens to be in a pub if it means I can kiss Dave? Heck no!

I lean in and whisper, "You know what, I don't think I can wait so if the offer is still on the table, I—" And before I can finish my ramble, he puts his lips on mine. They are soft, firm, and demanding, and sparks fly throughout my whole body. I have never felt anything like it. I am floating. I am forgetting what to even do here because I am so lost in how it feels. It is everything I have ever wanted a kiss to be. It's like every romantic movie I have ever watched bundled all together in a moment. His lips press soft and then a little harder, and I slowly open my mouth to receive his tongue. He tastes like beer with a hint of mint.

The whole pub and everyone in our orbit disappear, and I am floating up into the night sky. It's a moment made for us to confirm that everything I have been feeling for this man has been real, that we are meant to kiss like this, forever. I had no idea chemistry like this existed, and it only confirms the pull I have felt for him these past few months. Dave seems to be feeling the same, as he claims my mouth like it has always been his.

I don't know how long we sit there on the bench seat by the window exploring each other's mouths, soft and hard and entirely us. We break apart for some air and stare into each other's eyes, like a knowing of what just transpired has just changed everything.

I rest my index fingers on my lips, already cold from the absence of his. His lips were made for mine. The world stands still as I stare into Dave's eyes as he stares into mine like he just discovered that the sun exists. There's hunger in his gaze. His hand grips my thigh and I feel the heat in his touch.

"Celeste, I don't know what just happened, but I think it's safe to say that we should probably get the bill and get out of here before we do something inappropriate." We both scan the pub, registering the people in this room with us. Seriously, did they see the sparks that just ignited and brought this restaurant up in flames?

Luckily, no one seems to be looking our way. I move to get out my credit card, but Dave is up at the bar paying before I have a chance. He comes back to the table and takes my hand, lifting me out of my seat. He grabs my coat and helps me put it on, then takes my scarf and wraps it carefully around my neck. His green eyes turn dark and promising.

I recover my purse while he puts on his coat, then he takes my hand in his and leads me outside. Before I know it, my back is against the brick wall beside the door and he is kissing me again. Our lips connect urgently this time, harder than last time, pulling, devouring. It's like I'm his air and he can't seem to get enough. Everything stands still. The city lights, all the traffic, anyone on the sidewalk behind us—everything disappears and it's just us, in this moment, knowing that there was before this kiss and after and that my life will never be the same.

We slowly break apart and grin at each other. Our fingers are intertwined, and he shuffles back a bit and turns so we can walk hand in hand in the direction of home. It's already dark out, but surprisingly warm, so I don't need my gloves. His long fingers curl around mine, holding firmly like he never wants to let go. We don't talk. We walk slowly while grinning at one another, and at every red light, we make out like horny teenagers.

There are probably about twenty stoplights we have to cross, and I have never loved seeing red lights more. Every time we kiss, it's different. Some are soft with quick brushes of our lips, and some are ravenous. I hold on to his arms, and even through his jacket I can feel the size of his strong biceps. Sometimes I put my arms around his neck to pull him closer and deepen the sensation. Dave wraps his arms around me, pressing his fingers into my hips and kissing me like he is starving.

Each kiss feels full of meaning. Who knows how we look to our fellow pedestrians, but I honestly don't care. I didn't know kissing could feel this good and this right. It's so natural, as if we were made to fit.

The thirty-minute walk feels so short, and neither of us want to say goodnight.

Dave holds his hand to my face and cups my cheek, now cold from the winter night air. "I don't want to say goodnight yet, Celeste."

I look up at him. "Me either."

"Shall we have another drink then?" We look beside us and up at the neon sign to the Frog and Firkin.

"Never been in here before," I say.

"Neither have I."

We enter through the large black doors to find red walls and plush red booths with some pool tables at the back. It's a Wednesday night, and it's empty with only perhaps two other tables of patrons. We find a private table off to the side and take off our coats. Dave goes to the bar for a pint of beer for him and an apple cider for me.

We sit across from each other staring into each other's eyes, lost in the moment. I reach out and touch his face. It has a bit of stubble from the day and I run my knuckles over it while he leans into my hand. "Dave, I don't know what just happened, but I can't believe how right this feels."

Dave stares at me for a long time before he covers my hand in his. "This feels like the most natural thing in the world. I have never felt this way before. To be honest, I'm having a hard time believing this is real."

"I know what you mean. It's like we fit, and everything just clicked into place when we kissed." I sigh. "So, where do we go from here?" Usually, I would be nervous asking something so forward this early, but I somehow feel confident in what has transpired.

"I don't know, but I would like to continue doing what we just did." He smirks and grabs my leg under the table, pressing his fingers into the outside of my thigh and squeezing.

"I would like that too. This just feels so easy. Like I have been kissing you forever, but I also haven't felt this kind of fire." I blush.

"Celeste, you let me know if I come on too strong, because I don't think I will be able to hold myself back." He squeezes me again, then begins slowly rubbing circles on my leg with his thumb.

"What do you mean, hold yourself back?" I laugh. "Please don't on my account."

"I feel like a whole different man when I am with you, and tonight changed something in me. I was always taught to behave with restraint, but after feeling what it felt like to kiss you tonight, I don't know if I am in control anymore. It just feels too good, so right."

I smile. "I know what you mean." I squeeze his hand on my thigh. "I feel this too."

"Well, how about we start with agreeing to never stop kissing, because I don't know if I will be able to at this point now that I know how good it feels."

"I can agree with that proposition, and let's make sure we are both up-front with each other if anything changes."

Dave grabs my other hand and kisses my knuckles one at a time and slowly moves up to the inside of my wrist. My whole body is combusting with need. This man turns me on in a way I didn't know was possible. And at the same time as wanting to launch myself across the table to have my way with him, he also seems to bring out my restraint. Like my boundaries have come back and I know my worth. I want him to keep wanting me, and I don't want to give in too early.

Dave walks me home once we realize it's getting late. Barely being able to disentangle our lips, we finally part ways, but only because we know we'll get to see each other in the morning. We exchange phone numbers and Dave asks if he can pick me up tomorrow morning. It's actually bizarre to think we both walk to and from work and have never run into each other. We figured out it has to do with him being a morning person and me being a leaving-at-the-last-possible-moment person. I have also learned that he doesn't have a car or even a driver's license, as he has always lived in a city so never needed one, but I have a feeling there is more to the story.

Once inside, I wash my face and change into my pj's. I fall into bed with the feeling of being on top of the world and wanting to pinch myself to prove that tonight happened and that it felt as magical as it did. I mean, I knew I had a crush on Dave, but the more we get to know each other, the more I appreciate how transparent he is. Because he always looks distinguished to me, I couldn't place how much older he is than I am, so when we discovered the difference was six years, well, that's not even close to a deal breaker.

I have been a romantic since I was a kid. When I finally got interested in reading, it was because of Elizabeth and Todd's relationship and the trials of *Sweet Valley High*. Then, when I worked at Blockbuster Video out of high school, I watched more than a normal number of rom-coms. I have always wondered if that elusive chemistry that I read about and watched even existed. Now, in just a few hours, I have experienced magnetism—how a kiss can have you so lost in the moment that the entire world disappears, a kiss that ignites every cell of your body with desire. It's like my heart has just cracked open to possibility. My imagination didn't fail me, it gave me hope for what could be, and that was delivered.

I finally drift off to sleep with a blissful smile on my face. When I wake up, I wonder whether I had dreamed it, but as I open my eyes and look at my phone to check the time, there is a text from Dave.

Good morning, beautiful.

I jump out of bed full of excitement. Last night did happen. I text back.

Good morning. See you outside in forty-five minutes.

I quickly shower and make myself as beautiful as possible. I choose an oversize yellow sweater and a pair of leggings with my black knee-high boots because then this way I can walk and look good at the same time. I grab my coat and purse and run down the stairs.

I walk out the front door of my apartment and there he is in all his glory. Tall, handsome, wearing a black trench coat and holding a huge black umbrella. He is sporting a smile that seems to be just for me, and I only feel butterflies.

"Should I grab my umbrella too?" I notice the smell of rain in the air. In Vancouver, you always know if the rain is coming that day, as the air is filled with a dewy fog and you can't see the end of the street. I am about to turn around when he grabs me by the wrist and says we can share.

We walk hand in hand to work and consider stopping to get a coffee, but now we are running a little close to being late, especially when we stop at every intersection to do a repeat of last night. We are a few blocks from work about to approach Oak Street when Dave brings up an important topic that hadn't even occurred to me.

"So, Celeste, I am new to the office, which means I am technically still on probation for another three months, and I am not sure how it would look if the bosses saw us together." My smile falters a little and I look down, not sure where he is going with this. "And I know that you have been there for five years, and I can tell from my short time working there that you are considered the office sweetheart."

My heart pitter-patters at the endearment. "I never thought about that. To be honest, I haven't even thought about us and the whole office thing." I give a small smile and tentatively ask the question sitting in my gut: "So, you don't want to see each other while we are working together?"

Dave stops walking, turns to face me, and looks me straight in the eyes. "Celeste, I don't think I am capable of not seeing you, not after last night, but I do wonder if we should be careful with who knows and how we act in the office. I kind of need this job and just want to make sure we don't give them a reason not to renew my employment. At least until my probation is over."

I realize he still wants to be together, and I let out a big sigh. "I can appreciate that and agree that maybe we should be careful." I grab his hand to keep walking, then continue my thought. "So, maybe we just keep this between us, except you should know Sophie knows, but I will talk to her today about keeping it quiet. Shall we only see each other outside of work then? When we interact at work, I think we can both be professional." He squeezes my hand in agreement just as we approach the hospital, then he lets go and I feel his warmth already leaving. But I do understand.

"Okay, so for now, no one can say anything if they see us talking, but we will probably have to be careful about touching each other, and I will do my best to keep my hands to myself when I see you around the office, but you better be prepared that the minute we turn that corner over there"—he points to a turnoff where the hospital is no longer visible—"these hands will be making up for lost time."

I give him my biggest smile because every time I feel any doubts creeping in, he seems to calm them instantly. We then turn and walk up the path to the foundation where I go in the front and he walks around the back. I walk up the stairs and wave to Sophie. In an instant, she points two fingers at her eyes and then back to me to indicate she's on to me, then yells, "We are getting coffee in ten minutes!"

CHAPTER 17 – DAVE

I can't concentrate on work. All I think about is Celeste. I still feel like I am dreaming and last night didn't happen because moments like last night don't happen to me. The way she looked at me, the way she listened to me like she truly wants to know who I am. I feel bad about leaving Paul sitting there while we talked at the pub, but I couldn't seem to look away from her, and he seemed to understand the situation. *What is the situation? Is this what falling in love feels like?* I have never felt so happy and light and hopeful, and Celeste genuinely appears to like me just as much as I like her.

When we kissed, it's like everything made sense. It was warm, but electric; it felt beautiful and right. We talked about our futures. We talked about everything: I like cooking, she doesn't; she watches hockey, I don't; I love classical music, she likes '90's hip-hop; she worships celebrities, I couldn't care less. We differed on many topics, but we also had many things in common: We both love crime films and stand-up comedy, we both love hiking, and we both love dogs. More importantly, we both want children. We were both hurt, but we both were willing to try one more time.

I drift off and stare at the wall, thinking about that walk home, about kissing her at every intersection, her hands at the nape of my neck, bringing me to her. Being with Celeste is feeling excitement and tranquility at the same time, a certainty mixed with recklessness. I want to be with her all the time. All the time. She is all I think about. She's all I want. All I know is that I've never felt this way before; any hesitancy or fear I had has vanished. How am I supposed to get any work done?

Luckily, my boss scheduled me for a few meetings, so my day passes rather quickly. Even if I can't remember what's discussed in the meetings. Hopefully, I took notes, as my mind kept drifting.

Close to the end of the day I text her: "Meet you outside?" and get an instant response. "Yep!"

I practically skip out of the office. I see her down the street and walk fast to greet her: *"Sweet, sweet is the greeting of eyes."* We start walking quickly in silence, turn right, both sharing a conspiring look at the hospital, which is now out of view, and we almost throw ourselves at each other. Just standing there on the street, our limbs and tongues intertwined. I have no idea how long we stand there, but it's the beginning of the rain that finally has us coming up for air. We laugh together under the umbrella and quickly make our way home. We both hesitate, like we aren't sure what should come next, so I start. "I have to take Tibby out for her walk and should probably do that before the rain comes down hard."

Her response surprises me. "Can I join you?"

"But it's raining, Celeste, you'll probably want to get inside."

"Actually, I love the rain and would love to join you. I need to meet this dog too. I have to meet my competition!" She laughs and so do I because everything just feels so easy. But her concern is valid. I do love that dog.

"Okay, I will go drop my things and get out of my work clothes and be back here in fifteen minutes."

She gives me her huge smile and runs into her apartment building while I run home. I quickly get changed into some rain gear, put on my Wellies, and grab my umbrella and Tibby. When I get to Celeste's apartment, she has changed into some casual pants, a raincoat, and a pair of rain boots. I think this might be my favorite look on her. She immediately crouches down to say hi to Tibby, who is, as usual, indifferent. It's my only gripe with her. She's the most aloof dog you could possibly imagine. Every other part of her is perfect, apart from the aforementioned shitty recall. She's easygoing and loves to play, but not with people, only other dogs. Tibby takes Celeste's affection with reticence, but Celeste isn't discouraged. She just looks back up at me and says, "Now I get it. She is the most beautiful dog I have ever seen. I totally would have noticed you if you were walking with her."

The night before, we established that Celeste and I had never run into each other because of our daily routines. I'm a morning person and she sleeps in. There are two local convenience stores, and she goes to the one on Broadway and I go to the one on 6th. I shop at the Safeway, and Celeste goes to the IGA. We've lived a few blocks away from each other for three years, but we just didn't meet. However, we do go to the same produce and fish markets on 4th, but we've never caught sight of each other. To be fair, I usually go about my business without engaging in my surroundings.

Celeste stands and we both open our umbrellas and start walking hand in hand, and nothing has felt more right in life. "Dave, I had no idea I would find rain gear so sexy."

I laugh and secretly love the compliment. We walk to the park where I can let Tibby off lead and it really starts to pour, like that rain that shoots up when it hits the ground. Overall, we are pretty protected, but it is raining really hard and all I want to do is kiss Celeste, so I do. She leans into me, and our kisses turn so passionate so fast that we have to let go of our umbrellas so we can get better access and have full use of our hands. We kiss in the rain like one of those romantic scenes in a movie. We are both soaked and don't have a care in the world. All we want is this moment and more of it. Tibby strolls by a few times and I swear I can see her rolling her eyes. I have no idea how long we stand in the rain; time stops when I am with Celeste. Nothing is as important as the feeling of whatever is happening between us.

Eventually, the rain becomes too much, and we run to the tiny Arbutus Coffee Shop. Celeste goes in to make our order while I find a sheltered place outside for me and Tibby. Celeste comes out a few minutes later, wet hair plastered to her face, mascara running. Her cheeks and lips are red from the cold. She looks so beautiful. We sit and warm our hands on our cups while Tibby looks at me with disdain as she sits on the semi-wet ground beneath the table.

"This could be a story we tell our kids someday," I say without thinking, and Celeste simply laughs. I don't think I've ever made someone laugh so much. I have a particular sense of humor, truth through comedy I guess, meaning I'll just point out things I see in daily life and give my disagreeable, yet truthful, take on it. Some people seem to find it a bit brutal and cruel, because my take on the world is quite different from others, but Celeste sees the absurdity in what I'm saying and not the harsh truth of it. She sees me, and I feel safe to be myself around her. I play no character when I'm with her, and she seems to like the cast. We finish our coffees quickly. She has floor hockey practice and has to go. We give each other one more kiss and reluctantly part ways.

CHAPTER 18 – CELESTE

My first thought when I wake up goes immediately to kissing Dave in the rain. I have always loved the rain and how it makes me feel safe and cozy. As a kid, I would sit under an umbrella on the deck just so I could feel closer to the sound. So, making out last night and that passionately with a man who has not left my thoughts in months, well, I will be reliving that on loop for a while. Months that I second-guessed the attraction I felt. Months where I dreamed of kissing him, and last night was more than even my imagination was capable of envisioning. I felt like we were reenacting the boat scene from *The Notebook*. No boat or dock, but a park and a dog. Standing there in the rain, getting absolutely drenched down to my bones, and yet, I'd been hot. Our bodies melted together and warmed us up from the cold, hard rain. Slow and curious and hard and needy. I have no idea what we even looked like and didn't care, I was just there in Dave's arms and nothing else mattered.

There is still so much I want to learn about him. The little pieces he has shared about himself so far have me only wanting to know everything, like why he seems so serious and closed off at work, but when it's just him and me, he is open and giving. I know when we are together I feel wanted, and also safe. Like I can trust him.

I get into the shower and continue daydreaming. I feel so full and energized knowing this is real life, my life, and I can hardly wait to see him again. When I'm finished showering, it is still pouring down rain, so I text Dave and tell him I'll pick him up. Once I am parked out front of his building, I see him come out his front doors. He jogs toward the car and quickly gets in with minimal rain damage. He turns, and his eyes focus on me, green intensity that looks full of admiration.

"Good morning, sunshine," he says. He smiles, leans forward, and grabs my neck with his hand and pulls me in for a deep kiss. This really is the best way to start off a new year.

After we break, I start the car and turn on the defogger full blast because we can't see through the windows.

"Maybe next time I should leave the car running," I say with a grin as I pull out down the street, heading toward Broadway. Dave has his hand on my thigh, his thumb moving in gentle circles. I have never felt so ignited, and I'm not sure how long I will be able to only kiss him. I want all of him.

The drive is a quick one while we chat about work and how we're happy it's Friday. I turn in to the parking lot and find a spot close to the entrance, and as much as I want to kiss him before we head into the office, I know our colleagues could be arriving at any moment.

Once inside, I head to my desk and immediately check my emails. There at the top is already one from Dave.

From: dpenni@foundation.com
To: cchild@foundation.com
Subject: I already miss you

Dear Celeste,

As the privacy officer, I can assure you no one at work will be asking to read our emails, so I feel safe to send you an email on the company server.

Please know I have been away from you for a total of six minutes and I already miss holding you and don't know if I can wait the whole day to kiss you again.

I'm in a bit of a predicament. What do you recommend in this kind of situation?

Sincerely,

Dave

I grin. I want him and he wants me. Life is good.

From: cchild@foundation.com
To: dpenni@foundation.com
Subject: I miss you too

I could start all my days with emails like this. You should see how big my smile is.

I do know that the hospital is fairly large and that there has never been a reason for anyone from this office to go down to the basement. Would you consider meeting me on the bottom floor at 11 a.m.?

Yours, Celeste

He replies quickly.

From: dpenni@foundation.com
To: cchild@foundation.com
Subject: miss you more

I think that sounds like a delectable idea. I have
never been to the basement myself and am looking
forward to getting acquainted with the space and you.

Dave

P.S. You rock.

(And he has inserted a meme of a cartoon rock and
ruler, and the ruler is telling the rock, "You rock"
while the rock is telling the ruler, "You rule.")

I smile.

From cchild@foundation.com
To: dpenni@foundation.com
Subject: miss you more x2

Take the back stairs that no one uses, and I will
take the elevator from this floor.

Can't wait.

xo

P.S. You rule.

I switch my attention to emails from my bosses, then meet Sophie
and we go to Starbucks. I catch her up on the night before and how
surreal it all feels. She notices a change in me too. I am not questioning
myself like I did before. Some kind of confidence has come into the
scenario. I don't know if it's because I feel this instant connection of
trust or that I feel like he likes me just the way I am, but I don't feel
rattled or doubtful; instead, I feel like I am allowed to trust what is

happening and enjoy it. I feel like the Celeste who moved to Vancouver all those years ago, the Celeste full of hope and optimism.

We start walking back to the office with our coffees in hand and Sophie grins her big smile and pulls me down to sit on a bench with her. I give her a curious look, but she seems determined.

"Celeste, I need you to hear me." She looks at me earnestly. "You deserve this. You are one of the most kind, generous, and loving people I know, and I saw how Mike made you question who you were and your worth. And I am so proud of you for kicking him to the curb." She takes a deep breath, pulls my shoulders so I am facing her, and continues. "So please hear me when I say you can enjoy this, you can believe what is happening is real. And trust what you're feeling; trust your gut. If Dave gives you any indication that he isn't being genuine, then deal with it. But until or if that happens, don't look for it. Allow yourself to receive his praise and kindness. You're worth a good man, Celeste, and I think Dave is one of the good ones."

I lean in and give her a big hug. I didn't realize how much I needed to hear this at this moment. That I can trust what I'm feeling. That I can be honest with Dave and myself about what is transpiring and not look for things to go wrong.

It's only twenty minutes until I get to see Dave. I go to the bathroom to freshen up, check my breath, pop a mint, and head for the elevator. It slowly descends, and once the doors open, there he is, waiting for me with his hands in his pockets, leaning against the back concrete wall with his head down. I take a moment to breathe in my reality. This man is waiting for me! He looks up, and as he slowly scans me from head to toe, I feel hot all over. He pushes himself off the wall to grab my hand and intertwines our fingers, then begins kissing me. The doors almost shut on us before Dave pulls me closer.

We realize at the same time that we probably need to find a different spot if we are going to be making out. So, we begin walking through the maze of hallways, passing the occasional hospital employee. I spot one hallway that looks dark and hidden, so we walk about ten feet down the corridor where we find a little alcove with a door that has a padlock on it and looks abandoned. Perfect.

I pull Dave in and kiss him with all the want I have been feeling, trying to communicate to him that I want this, that I trust this, that I want to see what this could be. He kisses me like he understands what this means too. We are both filled with each other, this longing of finding something we didn't know could happen to us, that a connection this rare can also feel this right. This quickly.

We hear some footsteps, and I break our kiss to peek over Dave's shoulder and witness two men in maintenance uniforms walk by. They give each other a look but continue walking without saying anything.

I have no idea how long we've been here, as I'm just lost in Dave and his mouth and how good this feels. My hands are on the back of his neck, my fingers running through his hair. His hands are on my hips, squeezing and almost lifting me up. Then hands move over each other like we want to touch everything, and I feel him against my leg and shiver.

I break away panting when I hear some more footsteps and see another maintenance person walk by. I laugh a little and whisper, "Dave, I think this might be the hallway to the maintenance room."

He looks down at me. "And?"

"I think it means this might be a good place. There are no colleagues down here, and I don't think our office converses too much with maintenance, so maybe we have found our make-out spot."

He chuckles. "Our make-out spot. Celeste, do you plan to have your way with me down here?"

"Maybe. What do you think?"

"I think you could probably ask me to do anything right now and I would say yes."

I reach up and hug Dave, the biggest hug I can squeeze, and he hugs me back. Our bodies mold perfectly together. I feel his heart humming in my chest, and I want to keep this moment with me forever.

I check my watch. "Dave, it's eleven-forty!"

He chuckles again. "So, we have been making out for forty minutes and yet it feels like we just got here." He leans down and places a light kiss right beside my jaw. "Well, I definitely think this should be our new make-out spot, but more importantly, what are you doing tonight?"

"No plans."

"Can I make you dinner?"

I nearly swoon. This man wants to make *me* dinner.

"I would love that." I beam at him, and we stare at each other a little longer until another maintenance man walks by and reminds us that we really should get back to work.

We say goodbye right in front of the elevators. "See you in the parking garage at four thirty-one, and it can't come soon enough," I say just as the doors close.

I find a way to work the rest of the afternoon with only minimal daydreaming, as I know that I am not going to be able to hold myself back tonight. I want Dave too much, and we will be in his apartment with no distractions. I wonder if it feels too soon. We are moving at our own pace. It might look fast to others, but it's like both of us know and feel something that just can't be explained yet.

When I meet Dave at the car and head toward home, his hand is on my thigh again, and he's doing those little circles that light me up. It makes it hard to focus on the road.

"I need to pick up some groceries. Do you have anything you don't like to eat?"

"Nope, love everything, especially if someone is cooking for me."

"Great! I have a few ideas. Come over around seven?"

"Looking forward to it." I try to focus on the road as I quietly say, "And would you mind picking up some condoms?" I don't look over, as I'm a little worried this is too forward.

Dave's squeezes my leg and turns toward me with a sly grin I love so much. "You sure, Celeste?"

We come to stop at a traffic light, and I look him straight in the eyes. "I'm sure."

Dave's hand begins moving in tiny circles again, but I also notice it has moved a little higher.

I'm all nervous excitement as I have another shower. I decide to wear something simple and comfortable. I have never been someone who feels the need to dress up unless necessary; besides, we'll be at his place. I can't remember a time Mike made himself dinner, let alone made *me* dinner.

The last few days have moved so quickly and yet feel like ages all at the same time. It's like we have this unspoken understanding that we really have something here. It's like we both know that this is something real, something worth trusting, something that feels like forever.

I leave for Dave's with so much anticipation. I really want to feel all of him tonight and hope he feels the same way I do. When I arrive, I buzz his apartment and walk up the two flights of stairs. His building is very similar to mine, just a little newer. I realize he has only lived in the space for a week and am so thankful he moved out of his townhouse before he needed to.

Dave opens the door right before I am about to knock and stands there taking me in. He is dressed up in a collared shirt, jeans, and a striped apron. He looks delicious. He grabs my hand and pulls me inside before shutting the door and putting me up against it. He kisses me like it's the first time, new and raw and full of all the anticipation of the night ahead. It's the first kiss we have had in private, which seems to have unleashed something even more.

We take a moment to breathe, and I look into his eyes. They remind me of a deep thick forest with sunlight peeking through the trees. The moment feels like magic as we stare.

Then my nose startles. "Something smells delicious."

He turns his head toward the kitchen. "Ah shit, the sauce needs stirring." He runs over to the stove and says, "Celeste, it's like my mind doesn't function when I see you."

My heart swells larger at his words as I look over his shoulder. "What are you making?"

"Chicken parmesan with roasties and green beans."

"Wow, that sounds fancy."

"Are you that easy to impress, Celeste?" He grabs a wine glass and pours me a glass of white wine. Looking closer, I see it's one of my favorite brands and wonder if I mentioned it before. I take a sip, taking in this new feeling of having a man look after me. It's foreign and welcome. "Well, honestly, I don't know if anyone has ever made me dinner like this."

Even though he has three pots going on the stove, his small galley kitchen is still tidy with the used dishes already washed. There is some jazz playing in the background, and I feel so good in this moment. I'm truly happy. I hope nothing happens to ruin it; I want to believe that this is what life can look like for us.

"Well, get used to it." He busies his hands, coating the chicken in the breading, then laying them in the baking dish. He looks comfortable here, easily stirring, cutting, and placing. I never thought a man in an apron could be so sexy. Or maybe it's the culinary confidence.

I take a moment to wander around his apartment and see he has set the table with two lit candles, brown leather placemats, and green cloth napkins. Everything looks like he took his time, like he cared. I look over the rest of his apartment and there isn't much in it, but it looks like he has already unpacked everything because there are books on a bookshelf, a framed photo of him and Tibby, and art ready to be hung on the walls. Tibby is lying on the couch on top of a dog blanket.

"Tibby didn't even stir when I got here," I say from the couch as I start petting her behind her ears.

"Yeah, I took her for a good walk so I wouldn't have to worry about her tonight, and she always passes out after I feed her. She is as nonchalant as they come, that one." He walks into the room holding a glass of wine.

"So, I have just put the chicken in the oven, and it won't be ready for another thirty minutes, so what do you want to do? We could watch some TV or play a card game," he says cheerfully, but his eyes say something different.

I stand, put my wine glass on the coffee table, and walk over to him. I turn my head upward and kiss his bottom lip, pulling it with my teeth.

Dave reaches behind him, puts his wine glass on the bookshelf, and grabs me by my waist, kneading my hips as he brings me to him in a passionate kiss. This kiss goes hard and wanting and communicates something fierce within us: a wanting that feels almost overwhelming. Our mouths move over each other, our tongues deep within each other, and our hands roam up and down and behind, like we can't get enough.

"Now, please," I try to communicate without words.

He walks me backward toward his bedroom and doesn't break the kiss. It's only us in this moment. Two adults, leaving all their insecurities at the door so we can be open to feel what is transpiring between us.

We start taking off each other's clothes. I fumble with the buttons on his shirt, and he takes over after peeling his apron over his head. When he removes his white undershirt, his chest is chiseled and firm, toned and strong, and so manly. I want to rake my teeth over every inch. Dave takes my sweater off over my head, and I reach behind and unclasp my bra. His eyes roam with wonder. His expression makes me feel cherished, wanted, and beautiful. He reaches out a hand and lightly strokes it along my nipple, almost making me explode at his touch. I take off my pants, leaving only my underwear, then remove his belt and then his jeans. He stands before me in his boxers and an obvious large swell hinting at what is to come.

Being with men before left me feeling vulnerable and a little insecure, but with Dave's eyes on me, I feel confident in my body. It already feels natural, like we have done this many times before. I feel safe under his tender looks and know that I can be myself.

We kiss and fall onto the bed with our hands exploring until I can't take it anymore and remove his boxers while he removes my underwear, then he reaches into his nightstand for a condom. He tears it open, his eyes never leaving mine, then rolls it over himself and moves over top of me. There is no other position I would want for our first time. I want to see him, and I want him to see me. He slowly and gently pushes into me, allowing me to take. I gasp at how right this feels. He starts to move, and his breath is in my neck while my arms are around his back, holding him closer. A tear escapes my eye. The emotions of this moment feel like a turning point, similar to our first kiss, but this one feels like confirmation. This is home.

CHAPTER 19 – DAVE

I wake up Saturday morning feeling incredible. Last night was better than I could have ever imagined. Experiencing that moment with Celeste, when we connected, I don't know how to explain it, but I just know I feel like the luckiest man alive and want to keep this feeling. That connection. When you find that person who makes you feel whole, like you always belonged there, right there in their arms, in their embrace, seeing her face smile at me like I was her whole world. I want to remember it forever. The more I am getting to know Celeste, the more I see how one of a kind she is. She is devoted, kind, compassionate, loving, sexy, and smart. Everything. Afterward, we ate dinner and Celeste was visibly impressed by the effort, and it made me feel good. We chatted for hours, drank wine, and kissed some more. We shared stories from our past and our upbringings, the conversation easily flowing. I wish she had stayed over but understood why she wanted to go home. I think we were both a little overwhelmed with how good it all feels and didn't want to push it. So, we have arranged to see each other later. She has a floor hockey game this morning, and I'm thinking I might stop by and see if I can watch. But first, I have to see the lawyer and sign the final paperwork for the townhouse. I am very much looking forward to that.

The meeting was quick, and I stepped out of the lawyer's office feeling like a free man. Knowing that it was the last time I would see Jenn helped with the feeling. This was a hard lesson for me to learn. I had compromised myself over and over again, gradually over time with Deirdre. Then, when dating, I continued to do the same: modifying myself to best suit the other person. But with this sale finalized, the profits I've received, and meeting Celeste, my future, for the first time in memory, is the brightest it has ever looked.

I head toward where Celeste plays floor hockey. It's way out in Point Grey. I could take the bus, but I've always preferred walking. Walking either helps me think things through or clears my mind. This time, my mind is buzzing. Everything seems to be falling into place, and only a month ago it felt like a life of filling empty time. The future is now full of light, full of happiness. A future with Celeste. I hope she is okay with me stopping by. I know it's a surprise, and I don't know how she feels about surprises, but I already feel like it's been too long since I've seen her.

I arrive and there are some bleachers situated right above the courts, so no one really notices me come in. I spot her sitting on the bench, laughing with her teammates. Wearing cute little shorts, an orange T-shirt, and socks with shin pads, it looks like she is about to play. The whistle blows and she is on the court, playing defense. Once the puck drops, she is on it, passing it to her teammate and running up the sides. The offense makes a few passes and scores, and they all embrace and jump up and down. They are so excited, so I look at the score and see they are down five to one now, so I guess getting a goal in itself was the exciting part. When her shift is over and she sits down, I see her eyes immediately look up and connect with mine, and she gives me her big Celeste smile. That's a good sign; it looks like it's okay I came to watch. My heart swells and I feel so lucky. I had given up on thinking I could find someone special. We hold each other's eyes and a wave of understanding passes through the moment: this is happening. This, us, and it feels so good. She breaks eye contact to whisper something in a teammate's ear, and they both laugh. She looks brilliant.

They ended up losing the game, but it didn't look like they cared. It just looked like they were enjoying themselves. I stand outside the front entry and wait for Celeste to come out. After about fifteen minutes I see her, still in the same sweaty outfit, and there is nothing I would change. She stops in front of me and grins. "Well, hello there."

"I hope it's okay I came to watch, I just really wanted to see you and couldn't wait until later," I say, hoping this doesn't come across as creepy, but Celeste soothes my fears.

"It made my day that you wanted to see me play. Hey, how did you get here? It's pretty far."

"I walked."

"You walked? That's like an hour!" She laughs.

"It was a nice walk." I blush.

"Dave, what am I going to do with you?"

"Keep me. I would."

Celeste grabs my hand and directs us to her car, but before we get in, she gives me a huge kiss, one that tells me just how happy she is to see me. I am glad I came.

She breaks apart. "Well, what should we do now? I am free for the day."

"I was thinking lunch on Granville Island."

"Hmm, what about my outfit? I think I should get changed."

I pull her tight to me. "To me, you look perfect."

She laughs. "What, in this horrible orange shirt that is way too tight and my sweaty legs that have imprints from my shin pads?" We both look down at her legs.

"Especially your too tight T-shirt." I smirk.

"Fine then, if you are okay to be seen with me, then let's head straight there. I'm starving."

CHAPTER 20 – CELESTE

He walked an hour to watch me play. It means so much to me. Mike had never shown any interest in anything I did, and here is Dave, after only a few days, showing up. He also doesn't seem fazed by my truly hideous outfit. Our team is the Crushers, and we wear bright orange shirts and matching socks. I am sweaty, and my hair is sticking to my forehead. Yet, he only looks at me. I can't believe he is for real. It's so much better than my imagination. When I am with him, I feel like I can be myself, like he wouldn't want me any other way, and it makes me feel strong, like the Celeste I used to know. If he doesn't care what I am wearing, then I certainly don't, and it feels good to not worry about trying to impress someone. I can just be me as I am.

I drive to Granville Island with Dave's hand on my thigh, and I update him on our team's winning streak. Or shall I say, our losing streak, but we do it with pride. Winning isn't really our thing, and we lose most games, but we don't care because we all really like playing and have lots of fun. He listens to everything I say, genuinely wanting to know. He shares about meeting with the lawyer and how he can hardly wait for that chapter to be closed. That is a situation that could logically bring up insecurities in me, but I don't feel any of them. It's like I trust him when he says it's completely over with Jenn, something that never really should have been. He doesn't even know why they thought it was a good idea to buy a place together when things had never been good between them.

We find a great parking spot right in front of the kids' museum and walk to the fish and chips place on the wharf. It's Dave's favorite place, and he orders for both of us while I find somewhere for us to sit. He comes and finds me and pulls my back up against his chest, his head on top of mine, just holding me while we watch all the boats coming and going in the marina.

"Celeste, I know it's only been four days, but you in my arms feels like the most natural thing in the world to me," he says as he squeezes me even tighter.

I inhale his scent and close my eyes, wanting to remember this moment. It's like every conversation, every embrace feels so easy. Like neither of us have to put on any masks or play any games, we are just allowing ourselves to express how good this feels as we learn about one another.

We hear our food number being called and he releases me, but not before he kisses the top of my head. I feel like I am floating. My list of what I want in a partner comes to mind, and I wonder how Dave matches up.

Dave returns with lemons and vinegar, and I give him a face.

"What?" He looks alarmed.

"Where's the ketchup?"

"Gross." He laughs. "I wouldn't think of putting ketchup on these. These are the best fish and chips in town!" But he hands me both baskets and goes to retrieve the "gross" condiment for me.

When he returns, I say, "Well, get used to it, because I put it on everything. I always have and always will."

He mimics throwing up, then laughs. "Well, I am sure there are going to be deal breakers for us, but luckily, I can handle this one."

We eat in silence for a bit and then Dave asks, "So, speaking of deal breakers, you mentioned you have a list for your ideal man. How am I making out so far?"

I almost choke on my fry, but I am impressed that he isn't turned off by the fact I have a list about who I am looking for. "Well, the first two you have for sure, and so far, it looks like you might have a few others."

"Like?"

"Okay, remember you asked, and you can't judge me, because some sound a little vain, but here we are. So, number one, must have a good smile and good teeth."

"Teeth! Huh, most English are not known for their good teeth. Thank goodness mine make the cut. Or at least I think they do." He looks at me with an over-the-top ridiculous smile.

"Yes, you make the cut." I gently lean up and press a soft kiss to his lips. "Two. Must like dogs."

"Yeah, that's a nonstarter."

"Three. Must be kind. Four. Patient, and so far, I am getting the sense that you are most certainly both of those."

"I will be honest, patience is something I am working on, but I can say I will do my best. What else?"

"I think that is enough for now. I don't want you running away, and this isn't some kind of interview."

We continue eating in comfortable silence as we drizzle lemon juice on the fresh cod. I am not usually a fish person, but this is deep fried and delicious.

Once we finish and have licked our fingers clean, I stand, grab our garbage, and take it to the nearest bin. I return to him standing and holding out his hand to take mine.

"Let's go wander and get an ice cream."

"Sounds good." As I start to walk away, he pulls me back to face him. "Celeste, I don't feel like this is any kind of interview, I feel like this is easy getting to know you, and if you have nonnegotiables in a man, well, I want to know."

My heart does a somersault because he really feels too good to be true, and I don't want to think about what might change because this has been so easy, and my life to date hasn't usually gone easily. I want to enjoy right where we are, getting to know each other. I give him a soft kiss on the lips, enjoying that now I can do this whenever I want.

"I will share more soon, I promise. I just don't want us to get ahead of ourselves." I interlace our fingers and we start walking the seawall.

We wander in and out of shops and find the ice cream stand on the wharf by the water taxis. I order cookie dough and he orders French vanilla, and we find a bench to sit on and watch the pigeons by our feet as the sea taxis zoom about, picking up and dropping off passengers around the harbor. Yaletown sits on the other side of the water with sunlight beaming off the windows and reflecting back a beautiful sunny January day in Vancouver. It's like it wants to match my mood, or amplify it.

We sit and take in the scene before us. "Can I ask you a question?"

"Always."

"What's it like to be deaf in one ear? You never say much about it, but I realize you always have me on your right side."

"Ah yes, that's so I can hear you better and not have to crane my neck." He pauses. "To be honest, I don't really think much about it. I was born this way, and when I was young, I had some issues with my other ear, so I think I am just thankful that I can hear at all."

"Was that scary when you were young?"

"Yeah, a little. There were a lot of doctors' appointments for a while, between my ears and eyes. So really, I am just happy I can hear your voice. I find it soothing." He grins at me.

"Yeah?"

"Yeah." He kisses me with his perfect pillow lips.

Dave has plans tonight to meet a friend and I am absolutely exhausted and would love to have a night in with myself. We leave Granville Island and I drop him off before heading home. But he doesn't get out before a very extended make-out session and promises of a Sunday together.

I feel like I am living in a dream. The more I get to know Dave, the more amazing I think he is. There have to be red flags somewhere. I am not entering into this relationship with my head in the sand. If anything, I am on high alert to see or feel mistreatment. But so far, he genuinely seems interested in me, is always honest about how he is feeling, and doesn't seem turned off by my antics. He actually seems intrigued by my quirkiness and constantly asks me questions about what makes me, me.

I also feel different. With my ex, I always had knots in my stomach when I wasn't with him. We had lots of arguments in our years together. Me asking him who he was texting, and him always giving vague answers. I sensed he was withholding things. Over the years, this left me more and more insecure and thinking I had trust issues.

I thought of the last time he'd left. I barely even wavered when he told me he was going to travel to Europe with his best friend, the very trip we had talked about going on together. He was so nonchalant about it.

"But that sounds just like the trip you and I always talked about going on."

Mike kept watching the football game on TV. He didn't even look at me when he told me that the timing worked for them both and they really wanted to make it a guys' trip.

"I get that, but I always thought it would be me and you going on a trip like this. You are basically going to the exact locations I talked about us visiting." I felt like I was pleading my case.

He just shrugged at me, then fist-pumped the TV and yelled excitedly when his team scored a touchdown. He then started checking off his scorecards for the football teams' point difference while I felt close to tears. I didn't reply, and he didn't even notice. He just switched channels to the other game.

I walked into the kitchen to see what I could make for us for dinner. Him going on this trip hurt, but what hurt even more is that he didn't seem to understand why I could be upset by it.

A few months later, he left for two and a half weeks, completely oblivious to how his trip made me feel: insecure, invisible, and alone.

After dropping them off at the airport, I returned to our apartment and completely broke down. I remember feeling devastated, which made me irrational. My mind wandered to all sorts of scenarios. I started looking through all the things he didn't take with him, including his phone. I wanted to see if there were any clues as to why I felt like such a low priority to him. And sure enough, there was a text exchange with a female coworker, someone he had mentioned in passing a few times but had never shared that they were this close. It looked like they texted daily and tried to get shifts together. There was nothing to say they were more than friends but for the fact that he didn't tell me about her and how close they seemed. Then, in his photos was a picture of her. The date stamp told me it was a Friday night when he had told me he was going out with one of his guy friends.

I slumped there on the floor of our apartment with my knees pressed to my chest, squeezing so tight I started to hyperventilate. I kept trying to catch my breath. I had never felt so insecure, so devastated. We lived together, and I thought we were committed to each other and therefore transparent.

For the remainder of his trip, I received a few email updates, but that was it. The whole time he was gone I was in a constant state of anxiety. *Will he hook up with someone else on his travels? Is that why he wanted to go without me?* I called my mom at all hours of the night to calm me down and soothe my racing mind. I stopped eating and cried myself to sleep every night.

My insecurities continued to grow even once he returned. He started tuning me out. I would ask questions here and there about his plans and intentions, but if he planned to leave the house without me, he kept it brief. It left me to fill in the blanks on my own, which wasn't helpful given my colorful imagination. When the person you're talking to is evasive, you start adding in your worst-case scenarios, and somehow, I accepted that as okay.

However, in the moments when I am not with Dave, those knots in my stomach don't exist. It's like they have vanished, and I couldn't even retrieve them if I tried. It makes me wonder if my intuition about Mike had always been correct. Maybe when someone is trustworthy, it's just as simple as that. You just trust them.

When I am with Dave, I don't question him or myself. I truly feel like this is the start of something special, and I really hope nothing large comes to interrupt what is happening between us.

Sunday, Dave and I spent the day walking around the Endowment Lands, winding our way through the trails and holding hands as Tibby ran through the park chasing squirrels and playing with other dogs. It might be January, but when the rain stops and the sun comes out, Vancouverites make the best of it. So, we decided to have a picnic down at Spanish Banks. We dropped by Capers and grabbed some sandwiches and drinks and ate our lunch on a bench overlooking the inlet before walking out onto the sandbar. We took off our running shoes and put them in the backpack Dave was carrying, and we rolled up the bottom of our pants. The tide was almost a kilometer out, which gave acres of sand to walk out on. I watched Tibby dig in the sand in between chasing Dave through the tide pools, tripping over his legs. I wanted to pause the moment, feeling the ocean breeze in my hair and sun on my face. I was just enjoying the day with this incredible man.

It's now Wednesday, and I am at work trying to get through a backlog of administration because I was a little distracted last week and there is a pile-up. Every day this week, we have met in the basement in our little alcove by the maintenance room. We kiss and hold each other as long as possible before we separate in the hallway and make our way back to our offices. I always take the elevator and Dave takes the stairs. It's probably a good thing we work on separate floors so our colleagues don't see us leave and return at the same time.

Keeping this romance just between us feels critical at the moment, and not just for the obvious reason of Dave being on probation. I'm not sure what the interoffice dating protocol is, but it feels like it should be our own little secret, at least for now. It's something we want to keep sacred before we get the opinions and thoughts of everyone else.

I didn't get to see Dave Monday or Tuesday night, but tonight we are both free.

We walk home hand in hand every day after work, strolling along 10th like we have been doing this for years and not the week that it has really been. We both debrief about our days. Dave has been struggling to communicate with some of the Fundraising team. His role is to help improve their systems, but they are very fixed in their ways and are not always receptive to change. Because I have been there for so long and have interacted with every department effectively, I am trying to help guide him a bit when it comes to interoffice politics and give him tips on each person's personality so he can better navigate meetings. With others he comes across as terse, but with me, he is soft and open. I hope one day he can show this side to everyone else because at this time, I don't think my bosses would be very understanding of me dating the new guy.

Dave leaves me at my front door so he can take Tibby out, which gives me some time to tidy and clean my apartment. After seeing his apartment, I think he appreciates tidy, but there's not much I can do about the smell of cat litter. I wish I had a scented candle or something. Argh. I said I would make dinner, but the truth is, I'm a terrible cook. Dave arrives a little while later and quickly meets Max before I escort him out the door. If we get too comfortable, we will never leave for dinner. I drive us to White Spot for a quick bite. The location on West Broadway has an old-school feature in the back where you can order and eat in your cars. They bring a long tray and lay it across your windows where you place your food. I love it. I order the legendary burger because it's my favorite food, and Dave orders a curry.

"This is terrible," he says, pouting after the first bite.

"Mine is delicious," I say as I take another bite, loving how I am not embarrassed by my order choice or eating in front of him.

He laughs. "But it's not food."

I make a funny face and squint my eyes at him. "Well, not all of us know how to cook like you, buddy!"

"Buddy?"

"Lover?" I tease.

"That's better." His eyes narrow and turn serious. I'm melting from his smoldering stare.

"Check, please," I say through my last bites.

Dave actually exits the vehicle and goes up to the counter to pay the bill instead of waiting for our server to come. He then starts to clean up the tray and return everything back to the server station at an incredibly efficient pace. We speed back to my place. We barely make it in the door before we are tearing each other's clothes off. I have been wanting him ever since our first time, and I want to see if my vivid memory played tricks on me or if it was really as good as I remember.

I wake up in the middle of the night feeling hot and immediately realize I am cocooned in a furnace. Dave stayed over. After two incredible moments together, we both passed out, and here we are, still naked, limbs intertwined. Dave runs hot because I am positively flushed. I try my best not to disturb him as I make my way to the bathroom for a quick pee, find my pj's, and carefully crawl back into bed. Dave immediately pulls me to him, murmuring something under his breath like "honey snuggles," and I wonder if I will be lucky enough for this to be my new normal. The way he kisses me, the way we make love, slow and sure and like both of us don't want to wake from this dream. It just feels so right. I fall back asleep while remembering how connected I felt to him last night. It was different. Since I have been on the pill since high school, we decided to forgo condoms, both looking to feel each other even more.

If I thought the morning would be weird, it wasn't. I wake to hear Dave rummaging through the fridge and I grimace because I know there is nothing in there. He returns to the bed and sits down, kissing me on the nose.

"Your fridge and cupboards are bare."

"I know. I told you, I live off cereal and mac and cheese," I reply, hiding my face in the pillow.

He strokes my head, lifting my face to look at him. "Well, we can't have that now," and I feel my heart expand that he isn't turned off by my lack of domestic capabilities.

"I still have to take Tibby out before work, so how about I meet you at work today, but make sure your calendar is open for our scheduled basement meeting." He gives me a huge greedy kiss, letting me know exactly what is coming later today.

Dave leaves and I lie there feeling content. I finally understand the feeling of what making love is. I get up, get ready, and head in to work, feeling like I'm walking on cloud nine.

CHAPTER 21 – DAVE

I have always struggled to get along with coworkers, especially those in positions above mine. Maybe I've attached too much meaning to corporate titles. Like I assume if you're a manager or director or something, then you have the ability to run whatever department you're running. You have the ability to effectively make decisions that produce the best results for your department and bring out the best in your team. If you're a VP or whatever constitutes senior leadership, then you have that next-level skill set and can see beyond the departmental level. You can see how all the moving parts work together and consider multiple facets of issues occurring both inside and outside the organization. Nonprofit is not like that, and it's my own fault for making such lofty assumptions of people and their abilities. In the nonprofit sector, in my experience, it's simply time put in. I've worked with a half dozen charitable and nonprofit organizations, and I can count on one hand how many people impressed me and still have a couple of fingers left over.

I've never been able to stand a lack of accountability, in all aspects of my life. I'm the first person to put their hand up and say, "My bad." Whether I missed a deadline or simply made a mistake for whatever reason. I acknowledge it, I apologize for it, and I ensure it does not happen again. And in the nonprofit sector, accountability is even more crucial. I could have worked for a bank or an insurance, distribution, or manufacturing company, but if I'm going to sit at a desk all day entering, querying, importing, and exporting data sets, doing the most mundane work imaginable, I may as well do it to help make something better rather than simply improve a corporate bottom line. Whether it's a little old lady putting a twenty-dollar check in the mail that she really can't afford, or a twenty-million-dollar transformative gift, it all runs on donations. Other people gave us their money. They gave it to us. So, I believe, because of the nature of our revenues, we should have a higher standard toward making sure that as much money as possible goes to the project and is not lost within the administrative process of handling the donation.

So, how does one achieve this? Efficiency. How can we determine if we are doing things efficiently? Data. Every other industry and sector seems to recognize this and will invest substantial amounts to ensure their organizations are run to the best of their ability. Not the nonprofit sector, in my experience. The solution here, similarly to the public sector, is to hire more staff to do the work rather than make the work more efficient. Sometimes, they hire someone like me to identify gaps in the system and help make them more structurally efficient, which is great. But then I am stonewalled at every turn as I attempt to make the changes they need when it is recognized that change is required. The catchword is "change management." A fancy phrase for someone like me helping guide people through a change in process. But I can't guide people who refuse to change, especially when there are no repercussions if they don't. They think I am being adversarial, but I am stepping in on behalf of the donor to ensure that their donation is being utilized in the best possible way. And that is important to me. Needless to say, this creates substantial frustration on my end and sometimes that frustration boils over, and according to Celeste, I don't hide that frustration very well. Apparently, I have "a face" or "a demeanor" or "a tone" that is considered hostile in meetings. I think "hostile" is a bit strong. "Contrary" maybe, possibly "belligerent" at times. So, it's crucial that Celeste and I keep things very quiet about our relationship, not only because I'm still on probation but also because the office sweetheart is involved with the office asshole. It is quite clear that few in the leadership team like me. Luckily, I don't care, but we have to tread carefully.

Celeste and I spend every spare moment together. It's only been a week and we should probably slow it down a little, but it doesn't seem like that is our pace. I am becoming more and more outspoken about how I feel, and Celeste soothes any fears that come up. I know now that I am falling in love with Celeste, but it is more than that. I am also falling in love with myself, with this version of me that only comes out when I am with her. People think we fall in love with the other person, and we do, but we also fall in love with the version of ourselves that is reflected back to us when we are with them. Sometimes we are lost through past fears, regret, anger, or loss, but another person can come along and see our true self and reflect it back to us as acceptance, as self-love, because they love your true self. They are the spark that ignites that love within, that truer, freer version of you. Celeste is my spark.

I make my way up to the second floor and peek my head into the office, and as six pairs of eyes look my way, I have a feeling that Celeste and I are not being nearly as discreet as I thought.

"Is anyone up for coffee?" I suggest, asking the room even though I don't care if the rest come or not.

Sophie speaks first. "I've already got mine, but Celeste?"

Simon just turns in his chair with a glare and doesn't say anything, so I am hoping that means he won't come.

Celeste chimes in. "Great timing, Dave, I was just heading there. Simon, what about you?"

Just say no, Simon, you grumpy little turd.

Simon grumbles, "Nope, go ahead."

"Okay, can I bring you back something?" she asks.

"Sure."

At times, I feel Celeste is too nice for her own good and gets taken advantage of. Let Simon get his own coffee. He could use the exercise. Celeste goes to her office, grabs her purse, and we descend the back stairs. I get a small moment where I place my hand on her back and quickly spin her to give a soft kiss before we exit the doors.

Celeste grins and swats my hand away. "Dave!"

"I can't seem to keep my hands off you when I am with you."

"Office stairwells have very good chances of our colleagues catching us, so you better behave."

Changing subjects as we walk down the open corridors that link all the buildings, I say, "So what is Simon's deal?"

"Oh, you caught that, eh? Well, Simon and I have always gotten along super well, but ever since you came around, he has been closed off a little. I don't understand why he could care. I mean, I guess he has figured out I have a crush on you and that has taken some of my attention away from him, but I'm not sure why he would care so much. He has a long-term girlfriend he lives with."

She really has no idea of her effect on people. Of course he is crushing on her. I feel a sudden urge to let everyone in the office know she is mine just in case there is anyone else harboring a crush.

We arrive at Starbucks, and we each order our Americanos and an extra for Simon. I still decide to pay for all three. Celeste fills hers with so much sugar and cream I don't think you can technically call it coffee anymore. Her diet is shit. It's all takeaways and sugary foods, and all I do is try to think of ways to get vegetables into her without her being offended. Though I do think the poor diet, like the lack of internet, is financially related.

We slow our pace back to the office and talk about upcoming meetings, and she gives me tips on the best way to approach them. She again brings up how in a few of the recent meetings, I have come across as "prickly."

"Yeah, but I don't care what they think of me. It's my guiding principle in life."

"I just want everyone to see who I get to see: this generous, kind man."

I shrug and furrow my brow. I've never been called generous or kind by anybody. But I do care what she thinks. "I will try, it just seems that they don't listen to anything I say, and every meeting is me repeating myself and nothing gets done. I truly don't understand why half of them still have jobs."

"Well, that perspective right there is not going to make you any friends."

"I don't care. I'm not here to be their friends. I need them to enter their activity in the database correctly so that my reports work."

"Well, if you want people to do as you ask, you have to ask nicely."

"What if I ask you nicely to have dinner with me Friday night?"

"I would say yes."

"Great, but this time I am going to cook at your place." Then maybe I can sneak some extra food into her fridge without her realizing my intention.

Wednesday flies by in a blur. On Thursday we have a staff meeting, and I sit across from Celeste. We both try to avert our eyes, while in reality, we just keep staring at each other. It takes everything in me to not look up and see her beautiful face with her swollen lips where I kissed off all her lipstick in the basement only half an hour ago.

By Friday, I can hardly wait to get out of the office. Celeste and I walk home together along 10th, strolling and holding hands like it is the most natural thing in the world.

"You sure you don't want me to drive you to get the groceries?"

"Nope. I have my old lady trolley."

She starts laughing really hard. "Your what?"

"My old lady trolley. You know, those large bags on wheels that you see old ladies pulling."

"Yes, but why do you have one?"

"It's practical. I don't have a car, and I like to make everything from scratch, which means I have a lot to pick up and it's too heavy to carry home. Especially when I do a Costco run."

"Costco?! Dave, that is like a twenty-minute car ride from here. You seriously pull that behind you the whole way home?"

"No, I take the Skytrain for most of it. It's only a few blocks' walk after that. Is this a concept that is really that hard to imagine?" If it were anyone else, I wouldn't be responding so politely. *What's the big deal?* This is the most hilarious thing she has ever heard.

"Well, you always seem to impress me, Dave. There are not many people that committed to getting their Costco purchases home who wouldn't have gone for a taxi." And when she praises me like that, any upset I was feeling quickly evaporates.

CHAPTER 22 – CELESTE

On Friday night, Dave makes me Shepherd's Pie, and it's delicious. He makes sure I keep all the leftovers and even bought extra peas for me to have with each portion for lunches. He also added a few new items to my fridge including yogurt, granola, fruit, cream cheese, and crackers, and even though I should maybe feel embarrassed by it, I am very appreciative. I feel cared for and looked after. I could get used to this.

It's almost like my imagination of what could be possible with this man wasn't so silly. I had felt a cosmic pull toward him the minute I saw him and then my mind took over with possibilities. I remember a quote from the book I am reading by Napoleon Hill: "Man's only limitation, within reason, lies in his development and use of his imagination." Perhaps my imagination has been a positive thing in my life and not a fantasy after all. I mean, Dave has been showing me so many incredible qualities, ones that aren't even on my list. He keeps surprising me with what is possible in a relationship, and it's even more than I was picturing.

Everything feels so special, and I don't want anything to change. I like everything I am learning about Dave. I believe he is really showing up as himself and not keeping anything back, which allows me to trust him.

On Saturday, Dave comes to watch me play floor hockey again. Afterward, we head back to his place. Dave makes us some sandwiches and then we leave to walk the seawall with Tibby, breathing in the salt air and walking hand in hand. Weekends are the time when we don't worry about work or anyone finding out about us. We kiss when we want, we hold hands, and we enjoy our time, getting to explore the different treasures of Vancouver. Lately, it's been fun watching all the new buildings and venues being erected in preparation for the upcoming Winter Olympics. The city is buzzing in anticipation, which probably contributes to January not feeling so gloomy.

"You know what, Dave? I like who I am when I am with you," I say as we stroll along.

"Have you not liked yourself before?"

"Not sure. But I do know I haven't felt this good in a long time. Sure of myself. That who I am is worthy of what I want."

"And what is it you want?"

"To not doubt how I feel about something or ignore what my intuition is trying to tell me. I knew for so long that I shouldn't be with my ex, that how he was treating me didn't feel good, so I tried harder, which made me feel worse."

"I think I know what you're trying to say." He squeezes my hand while navigating me over to his right side while we pass a group of people.

"So, with you, it's like I trust myself again. I have these boundaries for my needs that have just magically appeared. Being with you is somehow bringing back parts of me that have been hiding. I have appreciated how honest you have been about your past and your emotions. I don't ever feel like you are holding things back from me, which allows me to feel safe with you."

We walk over to a bench and take a seat, me on his right while Tibby lies down at our feet. We look out at the inlet, at dog owners below throwing balls into the ocean, and the sea bus coming to pick up another group of people.

"When I am with you, I feel like maybe I can have the life I always dreamed of, one that is full of promise. That, together, life won't be such a challenge. I had given up on that feeling a long time ago. When I broke up with my ex, I had fears that my chance at having children was over. I think that is partially why I stayed with him so long, thinking he was my only chance." I pause, thinking about my words but wanting to carry on. "But I also knew that I wanted to have a family with a man who wanted me too, who could actually take care of me and his family, and so I took the chance that maybe, just maybe, I would be lucky enough to find someone in time before my eggs dried up." *Shut up, Celeste. That was way too much information. You'll scare him off.* I look down at my feet.

It's quiet for a beat before he speaks.

"I felt the same way."

I stop and look up. "What do you mean? What part? Because that was kind of a mouthful."

I mean, being thirty-seven, I had given up that I would get a chance to have a family, and I do really want one. But I also didn't want to be an old dad," he shares softly.

"You're not old, Dave." I grab his face and kiss the side of his mouth tenderly. "Do you picture a big family?"

Dave ponders. "Well, I guess I would like to have at least two because I have two older brothers and we are really close, and I think that it's important to grow up with siblings. Siblings that know you, know your history, know when you're bullshitting and when you need comfort."

"I can understand that. It's like having someone else who understands your life in the same way you do. Shared experiences. When my parents got divorced, it really changed me and my life and how I viewed relationships, and I think knowing my brother went through the same things helps make me not feel so alone."

"That must have been tough. How old were you again when your parents divorced?"

"I had just turned eleven, and my brother was nine. Our whole world turned upside down within days, and every day since has been different than it was before. I had always been really close with my dad growing up, and had always been really important to him, but afterward, it was almost like he didn't know how to love me anymore. Then my mom was broken and has never really forgiven herself for being the catalyst, so it's like I lost both my parents." I feel tears in my eyes because it feels good to share this with Dave, to explain a little of why I am the way I am.

Dave holds me close to his side with his hands wrapped around my shoulders, gently squeezing like he knows I have more to share.

"Both my parents behaved so differently, like there was the mom and dad I knew before they decided to split and then the versions they became after they separated. I don't think they even knew they had changed. It was just what they had to do to cope. Being so young, I felt the change but didn't know how to ask for what I needed from them. So, I also became different. I did whatever I could for their affection, to be seen and to be accepted, and it didn't really seem to matter much what I did because they didn't seem to understand me and never tried to. So, I turned into a bit of a people pleaser, molding myself to whatever people needed so that maybe they would like me. I know it sounds pathetic to say that out loud, and deep down I also know it's not who I am and not who I want to be."

"How they treated you had nothing to do with your value, Celeste," he says sincerely.

"I get that logically, but my behavior changed as I grew up. But somehow with you, it's like I don't feel the need to 'try,' if that makes sense. It's like I can just be me." I shrug.

"I only want you to be you, Celeste. Please don't be anyone else."

"Well, good thing that seems to be the version I am with you." I smile.

Dave is so much better in person than the version that had lived in my imagination. I still feel like I need to pinch myself at times.

The rest of Saturday is blissful and easy. We wander the streets for hours and have a quiet dinner in Gastown at the Irish Heather, Dave's favorite Irish pub, before heading back to my place.

Tonight feels different. We can trust each other and what we are feeling. Every moment we spend together seems to gain more meaning about what this could be.

We haven't shared any I love yous, but it sure feels like it.

After a slow, lazy morning in Dave's arms, I leave and head home to get ready to meet Dallas for brunch.

Dallas sits down in the booth across from me, joining me at our favorite diner in Kits.

"Girl, you are glowing!" Dallas almost screams.

"Shush, you."

"I am not being quiet. Spill! I saw you at the pub making heart eyes at each other all night, and I left because I completely felt like

I was intruding. Poor Paul." She makes a funny face, and after the waitress comes by to take our order, she immediately cuts to the chase. "Okay, so how good is the sex?"

"Keep your voice down, Dallas. I'm not giving details, but I will say it's like nothing I have felt before."

"So, safe to say, it was better than Devon." She laughs hard at her own joke.

"Ha ha. We don't need to relive that nightmare, please."

"Sorry, you're right, back to Dave. But seriously, look at you." She waves her hand up and down my body. "Your whole body is vibrating, you are absolutely glowing, and your smile might crack it's so big. So, is it serious, like are you a couple?"

"We actually haven't had an official conversation, but I think we are because it just feels like it. It's so easy; it feels like we have always been together. We both share whatever we are feeling, and he isn't even scared off by my list and keeps asking if he meets the requirements, and the attraction seems to be mutual."

"So, no doubt a wedding and babies are on their way," she states as if it's the most ordinary thing to say.

"Stop it! I don't want to jinx this. It feels so precious, like it's all ours, and I don't want anything to ruin it, especially me getting ahead of what it is. It's not even been two weeks, and we are just enjoying getting to know each other. I want to take it slow," I say, even though in my mind it doesn't feel like anything has been slow for us.

"Whatever. Just remember this conversation so I can say 'I told you so.'" Our food arrives, then Dallas continues. "Tell me what you like about him."

"Well, I feel like I can be myself. I feel I can trust him when I'm with him *and* when I'm not. You remember how I was with Mike. If

I wasn't with him, I was a wreck." I take a bite of my food and after some thought, I continue. "It's like Dave wants to look after me. He has cooked for me twice and filled my fridge with food. I feel cared for." I sigh and add ketchup to my eggs. "And all of it feels like it is for me. When I see him interact with others from work, he comes across cold and maybe indifferent, but with me, he is always so thoughtful. I love how smart he is, and he constantly makes me laugh." I chuckle to myself.

"I can hear that in your voice. This really does sound like the real deal." Her voice sounds wishful. I think something is going on in her relationship, but she always says she doesn't want to talk about it.

"What's new with you?"

"Nothing. Same old. I am just going to live vicariously through you from now on." I lean across the table and squeeze her hand.

We finish up our meals and wander 4th Avenue, checking out the boutiques. Shopping has always been our favorite pastime, even if these days I am just looking.

Our conversation does have me in my head a little, wondering if Dave and I should have the relationship talk. Are we exclusive? We haven't made anything official. I know why we can't talk at work, but it does feel like we are hiding a bit. I think I have liked the hiding because it has felt like our own little bubble, but what if the outer world comes knocking? Would it ruin things? Could we handle it? I park any of my doubts in the back of my head at the same time as I get a text from Dave saying he can't meet up tonight because he has to go pick up the last few things in the townhouse.

Maybe it's good to take a day off from Dave, spend some time with myself, and make sure I haven't slipped into old insecurities. I am pretty sure that isn't how it is, though. It seems like I genuinely just can't get enough of him. So, today is a healthy break for me to enjoy my own company.

It's a cloudy, drizzly Monday morning. Dave is waiting outside my apartment to walk to work with me. Not seeing him yesterday made the day feel like an eternity. I spent it lost in my head, having doubts that maybe I have been romanticizing our time together, but seeing him here now, looking at me the way he does, all those doubts disappear. When I am with him, it's like everything in the world makes sense and that our two halves complete the whole.

"Hi, beautiful," he murmurs before bending down and giving me a slow purposeful kiss.

"Hi, yourself." I grin up at him.

"It feels like it's been forever since I saw you, and I didn't like it." He grabs my hand and interlaces our fingers as we start walking. "How was your lunch with Dallas?"

"Pretty good. I forgot that I haven't really talked to her much since the first night at the pub, so she was excited to hear how we have been getting along."

"And how do you think we have been getting along, Celeste?" He's squeezing my fingers.

We wait to cross at the light at Broadway. "I would say rather well, almost too good to be true, if you know what I mean."

"I know what you mean. It's like when we are together, everything just makes sense. I only ever worry that something could come along and burst our bubble." He holds my knuckles up to his lips and gently kisses one.

"I just haven't felt this good in a really long time and I like being with you so much that I worry that something might change this, and I don't want it to."

"I don't either, Celeste. This is new for me, and I'm not going to lie, I have worries creep in. But I also feel like we will handle anything that comes our way. Together, I already feel like we are a team, eh?" He grins down at me.

"Yeah, I do feel that, and I definitely like playing on your team."

That conversation was the closest we have been to defining what we are. And I feel confident in what we have, and it sounds like he does too. I keep repeating his words in my mind: *We are a team.* That's how relationships should be. Two equal partners. Another requirement that was on my list. Check.

The week continues effortlessly, just like the previous one. Walking to and from work. Taking breaks throughout the day to meet in the basement. Spending the evenings making dinner and walking Tibby. On Friday, Dave says he is cooking me dinner to celebrate the final sale of his townhouse, and I couldn't be happier. He seems to genuinely like feeding me. I am learning how to receive his kindness.

Around sixish, he brings everything over to cook a fish bake. He brings his own cast iron pot, his Jamie Oliver cookbook, and all the ingredients. He also brings Tibby with him, and I sit on the couch with her on my lap and Max at my feet while Dave prepares dinner. It feels like maybe this could be us, like this could be our lives.

I don't have a dining table, so when it's ready, he brings us each a portion and sets the plates with our wine glasses on the coffee table. It's absolutely delicious, but halfway through, I feel a little nauseated.

I don't want to be rude, so I try to keep eating, but each bite is just making my stomach turn more and more until I am running off to the bathroom to throw up. I'm so embarrassed. He put so much effort into this meal, and I am puking my guts out.

Before I know it, Dave has joined me and is holding my hair back and rubbing my back.

"I am so sorry," I say, feeling terrible.

"Celeste, it's okay. What do you think is going on?"

"I don't know. It just started when I was eating, but it really did taste good," I managed to get out.

"It's okay. I am just worried about you."

I flush the toilet and stand, but I'm pretty wobbly. "Let's try that again."

"No, I think you should lie down," he says as he leads me down the hallway and into bed, where he helps me get under the covers and runs his hands in circles on my back.

"I will be right back. Let me get you some water and an Advil."

Dave leaves and I hear him clearing the dishes and cleaning up, and I feel terrible all over again that he went through all that trouble and now I'm sick in bed.

Dave comes back, places the water and pill on my bedside table, then comes in to snuggle me. "Do you feel worse or better with me in here with you?"

"Better." I sigh.

I don't remember how long we lay there, but when I wake up in the early morning, Dave is still in the bed, both of us in our clothes, and I am so thankful he stayed.

I watch him sleep. He is such a peaceful sleeper, with light inhales through his nose, and one hand on his chest and his other hand on my arm. I slide open the drawer in my side table and open my journal to view my list. I read through all the traits I wrote down. I ponder each entry.

♥ *Must have a great smile* - when he smiles, I feel like the only person in the room

♥ *Must have good teeth (that's weird, but okay)* - white and straight, they add to his smile

♥ *Kind* - since day one he has shown me kindness and tenderness, and he is also considerate toward others

♥ *Patient* - he seems to find my silliness funny and always holds space for me to be me

♥ *Loving* - when he cooks for me and after looking after me last night, it sure feels like love

♥ *Must want a family* - it's been such a relief since we had this conversation; it gives me hope that we might have a future

♥ *Respects women and men as equals* - he seems to like that I excel at my job and can support myself; so far, I haven't had any indication that he thinks he needs to be "the man" in a relationship

♥ *Loves dogs* - ridiculously so

♥ *Hard worker* - starts his days at the gym, committed to exercise for Tibby, works hard at his job to be his best, then still wants to make me dinner and clean up

♥ *Tall* - yep

♥ *Confident* - it's inspiring how confident he is in himself

♥ *Respectful* - always

♥ *Happy* - when we are together, he seems happy

- ♥ *Can provide for his family* - I know he could, as he takes all his responsibilities seriously
- ♥ *Feels lucky to have me (that would feel nice)* - he hasn't used those direct words, but there are many that feel close
- ♥ *Wants to try new things* - not sure; I guess only time will tell

His eyes open after he feels me stirring, and I whisper, "I'm so sorry I ruined the dinner you made."

"How are you feeling?" he asks.

"Better, actually. I am not sure what came over me. Thank you so much for looking after me; I am not used to it and I feel bad."

"Well, I like looking after you, so please don't feel bad."

My heart does somersaults.

We fall back asleep after removing our clothes and shaking the sheets. We wake up and Dave takes Tibby out and I get ready for floor hockey.

Dave and I decide to go to Costco (because what new couple doesn't want to test their relationship?). I secretly want to treat him to a trip to Costco so he can load up on whatever he wants and not just what can fit in the old lady trolley.

Turns out, we do Costco pretty well together. He covers every aisle, and we pick up food for both our places. I grab some ready-cooked chicken, and he rolls his eyes.

"That's just lazy, Celeste," he says, half laughing but also totally serious.

"Yeah, well, they remind me of my dad. Whenever it was Dad's turn to 'cook,' he would buy one of these chickens."

Dave picks up a large package of chicken breasts that he plans to individually freeze in portions so he can prepare them himself. I really am not accustomed to a man who likes to cook and is also so good at it. It's a big turn-on.

On Sunday, we take Tibby to Spanish Banks and walk the sandbar. The coolest thing about the sandbar is that when the tide is low, and you walk all the way out to the edge, you feel like you are in the center of the ocean. You're kilometers away from the city, and when you look toward it, it feels like you could walk the whole way there. It's a fantastic illusion. It's a sunny day, and we take our time, walking for hours and watching Tibby run and dig in the sand. I feel so good. It's another day to hold in my memories forever.

We are exhausted when we get home, so we order Indian food and then I head home so I can wake up at my own place to get ready for work. But every night that we part feels strange. It's the nights we stay over at each other's place that feel more natural. I walk home that night feeling strong and full of hope.

Today has been slow at work, so I decide to head down to the kitchen to make myself a green tea. I am not usually a tea drinker, but I don't want caffeine this late in the day, and green tea is supposed to be healthy.

I bring it back to my desk and slowly sip it, but halfway through my mug, my stomach starts to turn again. I let the feeling pass and then go for another sip, and the same thing happens. That's strange. Green tea has never made me feel like this before.

I am now feeling a little nauseated, but why? This sensation in my gut starts triggering some wild thoughts, but it's almost like something inside me knows something is different. It reminds me of how I felt on Friday after Dave's fish bake.

I do a quick Google search about feeling nauseated when drinking green tea, then watch the results upload. There is one response that intuitively hits. *This is just your active imagination, Celeste.*

I now feel really sick. It couldn't be possible. We have been careful. I know we stopped using condoms, but I am on the pill. I read up on the efficacy of the pill and find stories that state, although rare, it is possible to get pregnant. I run to the bathroom and throw up.

I need to get home.

I tell Dave that Dallas wants to meet up after work, so I'll call him later. I email my bosses and tell them I'm not feeling well and am heading home early. This is something I need to figure out on my own. I need to know if this is real or something in my head.

I walk home, grabbing two pregnancy tests on the way. I feel numb. I am terrified. Things had been going so well with Dave, and now it could all blow up in my face. We barely know each other, so why would he want a baby with me? All my doubts come roaring back.

I just need to know. I run up the stairs to my apartment and do the first test. It is a little harder to pee on command than I expect, but I manage. I sit and wait, rereading the instructions over and over to make sure I did it correctly. *Have I just ruined everything?*

The timer dings, and with trembling fingers I hold up the stick. Two bars. What the fuck! I squint my eyes. Are there really two? Yep, there are two. How is this happening? Okay, maybe it's a false positive. I head to the kitchen and get a glass of water while taking some deep breaths. Okay, I will do the other test just to make sure before I have an official freak-out.

Test number two, two lines again. I feel sick and puke until I have nothing left.

I knew that I would ruin this somehow. It was all too good to be true, and I should have known it couldn't last. I don't get to be happy. I go to bed feeling numb. I don't feel prepared to tell Dave. I lay in bed staring at the ceiling. This is all my fault. I mean, I am on the pill and usually always remember to take them on time, but what man wouldn't think I did this on purpose? Or what if he thinks I am sleeping around? There is just so much that is wrong; we never even got a chance to see what we could be.

Throughout the evening I hear my phone ping with incoming texts, but I can't even look at them. I have never been good at hiding my feelings, and if I reply, I know I will say something. I just can't think of him right now. I need to think of myself and how I feel about this pregnancy. I don't even know how I feel or what to do. I know I've always wanted to be a mom, but I thought I would be married and then we would purposely be trying to have kids, a decision we both made.

We just started dating. It's been three carefree weeks of hanging out, and now suddenly we have one of the biggest decisions of our lives to make. Of course it's going to change things, but does it change for the better or worse? Do we lose everything we started?

Am I ready to be a mom? I know I can't support a baby on my own. I mean, I can barely feed myself right now. I am barely paying my bills. Will I have to move home? There is no way Dad will take me in. Mom probably will, but is that how I want to raise a child?

I mentally make note of what I need to do when I wake up in the morning. One: must call in sick to work. Two: must make a doctor appointment.

CHAPTER 23 – DAVE

I wake up Wednesday morning and take Tibby to the beach a bit earlier than usual. Celeste still hasn't responded to any of last night's texts, which is strange. It doesn't feel like something she would do, but then again, we have only known each other a few weeks. Just as I am about to leave the apartment, I get quick text from her: "Not feeling good and won't be at work today."

I send her a text immediately and ask if she is okay, but she doesn't respond. I want to go over and check on her, but I don't want to wake her up if she is sleeping.

I decide to ride my bike to work, but I don't enjoy the ride. Work doesn't feel the same without her here. I send her a few texts through-out the morning and finally hear back around noon.

"I'm okay. Just needed a day."

"Is there anything I can bring you?"

"You don't need to bring me anything, but could you come over later? There is something I need to talk to you about."

I stare at my phone for a long time before texting back that I'd be there. I'm not liking the text, and my mind starts reeling. My first thought is that I have done something wrong and that she is breaking up with me. This doesn't feel like her. I go over the last few days in my mind and I can't recall any conversation or moment that would drastically change anything, at least from my perspective. Cold feet? Maybe she decided it's too soon to start another relationship.

Work can't pass fast enough. I have to know now what's going on. I leave work as soon as I can, riding as fast as I can. I head straight to Celeste's; Tibby can wait. I'm worried. Celeste lets me in. She looks a little pale, and her eyes are a bit swollen. *Oh shit, she doesn't look good.* Maybe she's just sick and that's that. I take off my shoes and follow her as she sits on the couch. I sit across from her and hold her hand, and she barely meets my eyes.

"Celeste, you okay?" I ask softly.

Tears begin falling down her cheeks, and I reach up to brush them away with my thumbs. Her bottom lip is trembling. "Celeste, it can't be that bad, just tell me what is going on. Whatever it is, it will be okay," I say while continuing to hold both her hands.

She looks up at me and says, "Dave, I don't even know how to tell you this."

My stomach sinks again. This is more than just being sick. Now I'm really worried. I just keep staring at her. She takes a deep breath and meets my eyes. "I'm pregnant," she says and takes her hands from mine and covers her face. She sobs.

I just sit there. My chest tightens, stomach drops, and palms sweat. My mind has so many thoughts going through it. We just met. I don't even own a home. I just started a new job. There are so many things wrong with this happening right now. I can't even process what she just said, so I struggle to find something to say. I have no idea how much time has passed before I quietly ask, "Do you know for sure?"

She looks horrified by my response, but we have only been sleeping together for two and a half weeks, so this just seems so unlikely.

"All I know is that yesterday when I drank some green tea I felt sick, the same kind of sick I felt on Friday night after the fish, so I googled green tea and nausea and 'pregnancy' came up as a possible reason, so I bought two pregnancy tests last night and they both said positive. I have an appointment with my doctor for tomorrow so I can be sure." She starts crying again.

"I don't know what to say" is all I can get out. My first response, emotionally, inside, is joy. This is what I've always wanted. I'm going to be a dad. I visualize bath times, first steps, bike rides, Christmas concerts, birthday parties. Then my mind takes over with the financial and the logistical. *How am I going to afford a home in Vancouver? Do we move out of the city? Then I'll be commuting all day. I won't be home enough. I need to make more money. I can get a second job, do consulting evenings and weekends. I can make it work. Holy shit, I don't even know how to fucking drive. How am I going to do this?* I know that I should probably be comforting her at this time, but I'm in a mental tailspin and attempting to collect myself.

"Me either. I know this makes no sense. We haven't even been together long. But please know, *please* believe me when I tell you I have not been with anyone else and I could swear I've been responsible for taking the pill, but I guess maybe I wasn't," she says, looking so scared.

"Of course. I know that. Don't think like that."

"Well, I don't know what to think. I know I am scared. I know I didn't plan for this, but I also don't want to make any decisions until I see the doctor."

"Um, okay. I guess I should go then. I have to take Tibby out. I haven't gone home yet."

She studies my face. "Okay, well, why don't you take the night and think about how you feel if this is really happening, and I will do the same. And Dave . . . I am really sorry."

I don't know why she would be sorry, but I don't say that.

I'm still numb. I just stare blankly at her and then stand up. So many emotions are flying through me, and I've never been comfortable with my emotions. I try not to deal with them. I want to hold her. I want to tell her that everything will be okay, but how can I? She doesn't want me to be there tomorrow. She will make the decision and let me know. There's nothing more to say, so I get up and walk to the door.

Celeste follows me. I put on my shoes and when I am upright again, I hold out my arm and Celeste steps into me and I hold her. We don't say anything. We just stand there, holding each other. I kiss the top of her head and pull away and reach for the door without looking back.

I get home, don't even bother getting changed, and take Tibby out. I forget to make dinner, and when my stomach growls at ten, I make some toast and then lay in bed. *Why didn't she call me the moment she found out? Why didn't she ask me to come with her to the doctor's office? Does she not want me there? Why? Stunned. What if Celeste doesn't want to keep the baby? What if Celeste wants to have it, but not with me? Can I provide for her and the child? What will work say when they find out? Do I have any say in what happens?* All I know is that I want this baby and want to be with Celeste. I also know that it's not up to me. I finally fall asleep, but it's short-lived and I end up sitting at about 3 a.m., waiting to go to work.

CHAPTER 24 – CELESTE

I am exhausted. I didn't really sleep because after Dave left, I felt even worse. I couldn't gauge his reaction or how he was feeling. I know he said he wanted to have a family, but it doesn't mean he wants that with me, or right now.

I keep seeing his face and how distant it looked. I really have no idea what he is feeling, and I'm scared that I might have ruined what we've just started.

The one good thing that happened last night is that I now know what I want to do. If I find out today that I am indeed pregnant, I know I want to keep it. I hope Dave wants to keep it too, and I guess we can find a way to co-parent even if we aren't together. I feel scared but also confident—confident in my decision and confident I will make a great mother. I know I will figure this out, even if I am alone. I always do.

I don't see Dave at work in the morning. I had texted him that my appointment was at one and that I would let him know when it was done. Then I would meet him across the street from the hospital. I appreciate that he didn't ask to come. For some reason, I need to do this on my own. My doctor's office is within walking distance from work, so I am able to fit the appointment in at lunch and no one at work has to know where I am going.

When I arrive, the nurse sends me to pee in a cup and then leads me to a small waiting room where I wait.

It feels like forever until she comes in through the door, and I am holding my breath. I want her to tell me it's positive; I know in my heart I want this baby.

The doctor shuts the door and immediately gets to the point.

"Okay, Celeste, I have your results, and it looks like you're going to be a mother," I hear as she beams at me and then keeps talking about follow-up appointments and asking questions about my current lifestyle. She hands me a bunch of papers with things I need to consider like no coffee, no drinking, and what symptoms I might be feeling in my first trimester.

She asks me when I had my last period, and after looking at my pill packet and counting backward and comparing it to the calendar, I tell her it started on January 4, and she lets me know that technically, that would be the day I got pregnant. This means I am three weeks.

"Isn't this really early to get confirmation on being pregnant?"

"It is a little uncommon, but the hormones are present, the tests picked up on it, and you are most certainly pregnant," the doctor says. "It's actually great your body knew so quickly because now you can start taking the prenatal vitamins and stop the caffeine. You're a great age, and I am sure this will be a healthy baby."

"It kind of came as a shock. I wasn't expecting this news," I say.

"You should also know there are a lot of resources to help single mothers," she says while looking at my chart like it's no big deal. She looks up and when she sees me grimace, she adds, "I just saw on your file that you're not married, but please know, women do this all the time without a partner."

"Thanks," I say, not really wanting to get into the details of my current situation and why I showed up at the appointment alone.

"Celeste, you're a healthy woman, and I am sure this will be a healthy pregnancy. I see nothing to be concerned about," she declares, and it does feel good to have her say that.

"Thank you. I appreciate you seeing me at the last minute. I just needed to know for sure."

"Totally understandable. You do have a lot of next steps to do and appointments to make, but Nancy at the front will fill you in on those details. Anything else?"

"No, thank you," I say as she steps out of the room to her next patient, and suddenly I'm alone. And pregnant.

At reception, I book all the follow-up appointments needed for the next few months, and it's good she wants to see me again next week because I don't think I retained anything she shared with me today.

I start walking back to the hospital and text Dave that I am on my way. He texts that he will meet me at the park on 13th. For January, it is a warm day, so I have my coat open and hands bare.

Each block I walk solidifies that this is right, that I want this. I really hope Dave wants the baby and maybe even me too. It might feel quick, but I know how I feel about him, and I know we are good together. I know that everything has felt easy with him since our first date and remember that our first non-date was on January 5, which means that I technically got pregnant before our first date. I start laughing out loud because you can't make this shit up. It makes me think that this little love growing inside me knew what they were doing somehow. I know I am supposed to be with Dave, and I know we can figure this out as we go, and I just pray that he feels the same way.

I take a left off Heather Street and there, standing tall and handsome as ever, is Dave. He has a bag in his hand and his back is turned to me, so he doesn't see me approaching, and I still think he is the best-looking man I have ever seen. I want to run into his arms and kiss him senseless. My body feels light and hopeful even though I still don't know how he feels about everything.

I am a few feet away when he turns and takes me in. We stand about three feet apart and just stare at each other, his green-and-golden eyes creased with worry. I give him a small smile and nod my head in confirmation.

"I am pregnant, and you should know that I want to keep it. And with that said, I don't expect anything from you, and I don't want you to feel pressure if you don't feel ready to be a dad or be with me," I say confidently because I feel calm and sure, and I don't want him to be with me out of obligation.

Dave's eyes open wide, and he holds his hand out for me to walk to him. He pulls me in and hugs me tightly, and I take a long inhale of his scent because it feels like it was made for me, but I also want to remember it in case this is the last time I get to be this close. He pulls away so he can look at me.

He whispers my name, holds my face, and stares me straight in the eyes. "The minute I saw you. The minute you smiled at me at the Christmas party, I knew. I knew you were mine. You are everything I ever wanted. I've spent my whole life in regret, regretting my past. Living with the mistakes I've made in my life. Stupid mistakes, but they were all worth it if they led me to you. Everything makes sense now, even this moment. I feel I am the person I am supposed to be when I am with you. This is who I am. For the first time in my life, I feel like the luckiest man alive, because I am, and I will do everything to show how much I love you."

I give him the biggest smile my face is capable of because this *is* my life. He loves me.

"Celeste, look, I know it's been quick, it's been kind of crazy, but it also feels right. I had given up on a family and now we are having a baby. To know you want to keep it, that we could be a family, it is everything I could have ever asked for."

I beam at him and notice the bag in his hand. "What's that?"

He pulls out a stuffed bear. It's black with a brown nose and paws. "It's our child's first teddy bear. I bought it in the hospital gift shop this morning. They didn't have many options, but I thought this guy was pretty cute." That means he bought it for me before I told him my decision, that he was wanting it to be positive.

He passes it to me tentatively, and I take it and hold it close to my chest. "Dave, the first time I saw you in the office, I knew you were meant for me. I can't explain it because it was just a knowing inside me that I hadn't felt before. That pull toward you is what kept me trying to get your attention through the fall." I hold his face in my hand. "I know it was love at first sight for me and then when you kissed me, it confirmed everything I was feeling inside. I am so in love with you."

Dave goes to say something, but I continue. "Dave, you are an incredible man. You are so kind, smart, and thoughtful. I know you will make a great father, and I feel honored to have you be the father to my child."

"Celeste, I love you so much, and I will give you everything I have. Let's go choose a ring; I want everyone to know," he says as he pulls me to him. I look up at his face and lean in for a kiss. The kiss communicates so much more than our words. It holds future promises and the feeling that anything is possible if we are doing it together.

"Dave, being with you feels like loving myself for the first time. I feel worthy of being loved by you. I trust myself again. I feel hope again. A promise. You are everything I could have ever imagined and more, and I will never take your presence for granted. So, I want to thank you for being who you are, because you are perfect for *me*."

"I know *I* won't always be perfect, that *we* won't always be perfect," he says, holding me. "I know that we will be tested, but I know we will get through it if it's you and me." He places a hand on my stomach. "The three of us."

"Wow, a family, just like that. Everything I had hoped for happened in a matter of weeks. You and me and now—" I look down and cover his hand in mine, then return his gaze. "Before I found you I was lost, and now when I look into your eyes, I feel found, whole, loved."

I stare up adoringly at this man. I wrote him down on paper just over a year ago, and here he is. Everything on my list has materialized, and more. My love list. My imagination was limited in what was possible. I manifested this man. He was always meant for me and had been waiting for me to choose me too so he could find me. So much can change in a year's time. Life really can surprise you, and in the best possible ways.

I have never felt more sure of anything in my life and can hardly wait to see what else this life has in store for us, because if we are in it together, anything is possible.

EPILOGUE – DAVE
ONE YEAR LATER

Tibby waits patiently while I finish strapping in Percy and put the rain cover over the pram. We bounce down the back steps and out into the alley. The rain is really coming down, but we all need some fresh air and Celeste needs some sleep. A few steps and we're at Alder Crossing. I always stop here for a moment and take it in: False Creek, the Vancouver skyline, and the North Shore Mountains beyond. I can't believe this is real. I can't believe I have this life, but I do. We walk the Island Park Walk, through Sutcliffe Park, past Granville Island, then under the bridge through to the marina. The rain lets up enough that I can pull the plastic rain cover back and let Percy breathe in the salt air. We pass under the Burrard Street bridge, past the Kitsilano Coast Guard Station through to Vanier Park. I let Tibby off lead to chase the ducks by the pond as we make our way toward the dog beach. I look out on to the ocean and the cargo ships and tankers there.

I take a deep breath. This is my life. Everything is working out. For the first time, things are easier than they have ever been. I didn't know it at the time, but I was manifesting everything I had been asking for. Admittedly, not in the way I had imagined, but everything I wanted was coming true. Considering the circumstances and the speed at which everything happened, things fell into place pretty much perfectly. The townhouse on Arbutus sold, and I walked away with enough for a down payment for a new home and for an engagement ring. I spent more than I should have on the ring, but I didn't care. I wasn't going to spend the rest of my life looking at that ring and thinking: *That's all I could afford at the time.*

A month after we found out about the pregnancy, we invited Celeste's family down from the Okanagan under the premise of meeting me, but in reality, to tell them we were starting a family. It went well, all things considered. Same with my family. Awkward congratulations were given, and everyone was happy for us. We had to tell our bosses that the guy everyone hates is dating the girl everyone loves, and we received the appropriate reception. The office baby shower was incredibly awkward; everyone was biting their tongues, and I knew it, just as they knew I didn't give a shit what they thought. Celeste saw me, and that's all that mattered.

Since I would be the one driving Celeste to the hospital, at age thirty-seven, I was finally able to drive a car. It all seemed so humorous to both of us. There were worries, of course, but no doubts, and in September 2010, I held my newborn son in my arms. Like for most new fathers, the emotions are difficult to describe, but it's obviously life-changing. The joy, the love, but also the responsibility. To submit oneself wholly to another human being is a humbling experience. You declare in that moment, on your life, that you will protect them from any harm: *"And through the fertile and waste, protecting, till the danger past, With human love."*

CELESTE

SEPTEMBER 2010

I allow my gaze to roam over this tiny bundle in my arms. There had been a flurry of chaos, but now there is just peace. A knowing. That everything unfolded exactly as it should, because in this moment, it all makes sense. Life sure does have a funny way of bringing you everything you hoped for. There was before, and now there will be a lifetime of loving him. Pure perfection with ten fingers and ten toes. He's fast asleep, needing his rest after a fast escape. This little gift chose us for his parents, and he made it known he would be joining the crew quickly. This is what it's all about: Love.

EPILOGUE – CELESTE
FOURTEEN YEARS LATER

I look down at my feet as I navigate around the puddles. Some are so large they spread across the whole road so you have to creep along the side using the bushes and tree branches to hold you up as you shimmy down. The boys are already in front of me doing their own little dance through the muddy road.

Dave turns and offers me his hand while we continue our conversation. "Celeste, I don't think we give ourselves enough credit sometimes. Look where we are. Look what we are doing. Look at the life we are giving our boys."

I stand on an unsteady rock and hop to the flat road in front, getting closer to our destination. Percy and William have already disappeared into the trail. "You're right, I don't always let it sink in, who we are and what we have become, because really, I am so proud of us."

We now enter the trail head, ducking our heads from the mangrove branches hanging low. We walk in silence for a few minutes until the trail ends and opens up to a white sand beach. I spot the boys at the bottom of the small embankment, walking on the sand that has emerged because the tide is low. I then look up and breathe in the sight in front of me. The lights from the setting sun sparkle across the ocean, the sky reflecting deep shades of orange, pinks, and purples. The beauty surrounds me, reminding me of fairies dancing. The ocean waves crash in a crescendo that makes me alert to its power and feel like a magnet pulling me deeper into this moment.

Dave comes up behind me and holds me tightly in his arms. "I love you so much, and I am forever grateful you saw me and chose me."

"I don't think there was much of a choice in the matter. We were meant to do this life together; it was just a matter of our timing syncing up."

Our fourteen years together have been one adventure after the next. What else could I ask for? A husband who loves me so much and has been holding me the whole time as we found our way in this world. Who would've thought that all our decisions would have brought us here: watching a spectacular sunset in Costa Rica.

Our first few years were about survival. Trying to find some roots to raise our kids and take a breath. The next stage was for grounding and healing. Discovering ourselves and finding balance. Then once we found our roots, we started creating. Deciding on what life we wanted to live and then making that happen. Quantum leaps. Manifestation. We became confident to consciously create the reality we wished for, the reality we envisioned. It's incredible what's possible for your life when you tap into your intentions, imagination, and energetic flow.

My soul knew in that first moment when I met Dave that we were two soulmates finding each other. That first night we kissed was a recognition of what we knew already, a remembering. That knowing we had within is what has given us the confidence in each other and how we show up together. We had a lot to navigate right out of the gate, but over the years, we trusted our path. It feels like time has zoomed by and yet so much has happened since our integration. And here we are, stronger and more in love than when we met.

The list I wrote changed everything within me. I had clarity on what I needed in a partner, which gave me the courage to trust myself. Taking action and releasing what was holding me back allowed space for me to receive what I was calling in. I told myself that I was worth more, and the universe reflected that back to me. Dave also had declared the same thing. And it was delivered for us, plus more.

What I have discovered over the years is that what you want, wants you too. But you do have to match the frequency. If you have blocks set in place, the universe can't get through it. So, over the years, whenever we have manifested another opportunity or adventure or shift, it's been when we have let go of what didn't serve us.

The biggest lesson I learned was the power of our imagination. Most of us have been taught to make decisions based off what we can see or what we already know to be true, but when you dive into the power of your mind, anything is possible. You truly can create whatever you want in your reality, and that is exactly what we did. Over the years, Dave and I both leaned into opportunities that seemed aligned to our new life, including new careers. We followed our passion for traveling, eventually moving across the country, then back again. During the pandemic, we examined what freedom meant to each of us and as a family. We made the difficult decision to leave the country we had called home our whole lives to travel abroad. To see what else could be out there for us. So, here we are, exploring a country neither of us had been to, with our sons and our dogs.

When you surrender, detach, and decide you're worthy of having what you want, everything can start to find you. It wasn't easy, but it was so worth it. I'm proud of us, as a family, as a couple, and as individuals. Over the years and through our growth, one thing is abundantly clear: The first love you give each day is to yourself. We both became much better versions of ourselves once we learned to love ourselves fully. I also get the honor to love our incredible children. They have changed me and my life in ways I never could have expected. Our boys have extremely different personalities, and because they are so close in age, they are also best friends. They balance and nurture each other's differences. I have a hard time expressing my words for Percy because he changed our life. He is the catalyst to everything we have today, and I know he joined us intentionally. Percy is brave, smart, patient, and loving. And William balances us all out with his strength, radiance, charisma, and joy.

I lean back into Dave's body and feel his heart beating while we watch our sons make shapes in the sand. The kaleidoscope of colors in the beautiful sunset leaves me in awe and full of gratitude for this moment and for the life we've created and the love we share.

ACKNOWLEDGMENTS

Thank you for reading our story. I have been a hopeless romantic my whole life, always fascinated by people falling in love. But over the years, as I read countless romance books and watched countless romance movies, I never saw my story. I always knew it was unique; I mean, who gets pregnant before their first date?! I originally wrote it as fiction, but my publisher encouraged me to make it a memoir because this is a real-life love story. And I want everyone to know they, too, can find their one true love. The one they are supposed to do this life with and the fact that you really can know it immediately. I didn't include it, but Dave actually talked about looking for rings our first week together.

My favorite rom-com books have dual points of view, so I wanted to write our story the same way. When I shared it with my husband, especially his parts, he was like, "I would never say that." So, I feel fortunate that Dave wanted to share his perspective. He took my lead on what parts to share, but it's all his experience in his words, and I hope it added to the emotion of our story. Every moment, every kiss, and every conversation between us in this book actually happened. Thank you for joining us in our love story. I'd love to hear about yours, as I am a little obsessed with people living happily ever after.

Dave, I am thankful every day that you walked into that office. I saw your profile that day and I just knew. You were it. I'm grateful my colorful outfits didn't have you running the other way, and I appreciate how you have always seen the light that I am, especially when I couldn't see it myself. You make me laugh daily and bring so much joy and love to all of us. You're simply one of the best guys there is, and I will never take your heart for granted.

My two boys, your presence made our love story ignite into what you get to roll your eyes at today. Thank you for choosing us to be your parents. You will always be my why for everything. Never stop being yourselves. Love you infinite kabu.

Mom, thank you for helping us edit this book early on and for all the essays you helped me with in university. You being an English teacher and me being someone who writes backward, you always kept your patience, even when my dyslexia was prominent.

Sam, thanks for being my romance friend. You had my back when we were young and then again while you gave me really helpful advice as an early reader. You were only ever going to be who I trusted to see what I had written.

Dallas is a conglomerate of many of my girlfriends from Vernon to Vancouver. Each one has shaped my life in a way that is as unique as each of them. Some have lost touch but all were an important part of my life and for that I am eternally grateful. We had some really special memories that made our years together unique and noteworthy.

To Sophie, you're simply the best for putting up with my crazy shenanigans while you watched me fawn over Dave. And to all our other work friends who knew before the bosses did, we both appreciate how much fun you were having watching us. Dave having a sonogram picture up on his monitor gave it away to a few of you, but you all had our backs, which gave us needed encouragement when everything felt so new.

To the fEMPOWER family. Sabrina, thank you for trusting what I had written and then carefully guiding my confusing thoughts through this process. Kelly, thank you for your patience and encouragement while I did something I have never done before. Christine, thank you for polishing my words. Michelle, thanks for bringing my vision for the cover to beautiful fruition.

BIOS

Celeste and Dave were destined to fall in love. They knew as soon as they met, and their fifteen years together have solidified that every day since. Their union was just the beginning of inner healing, self-growth, and endless adventures. They both feel extremely fortunate to have found their soulmates and stay in gratitude for each other and for the beautiful family they've created. Currently based in Costa Rica, they continue to experience opportunities as they arise in their professional and personal lives and are excited for what's to come.

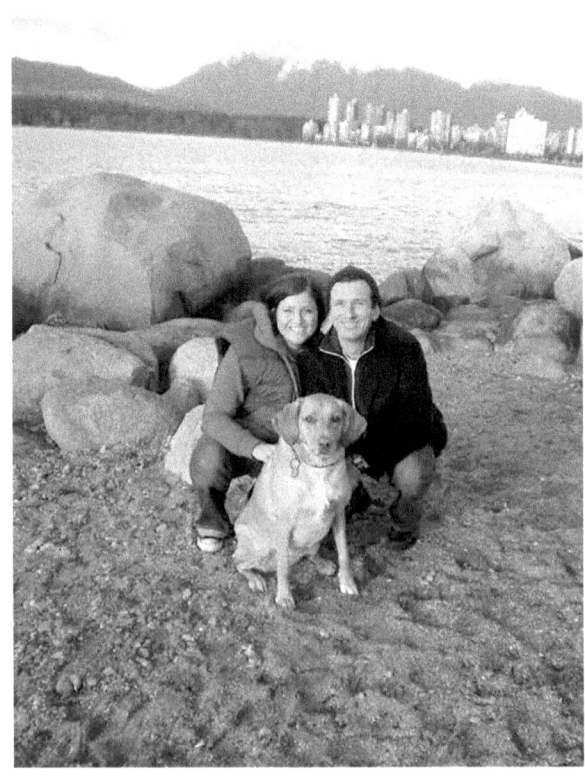

Visit us at

www.celestepennington.com

if you'd like to share your own love story

with us or follow along with our adventures.

At fEMPOWER Publications,
we don't just publish books—we amplify movements.

We support thought leaders, visionary storytellers, and creative entrepreneurs in transforming their ideas into powerful nonfiction books, journals, workbooks, affirmation decks, and personal growth tools that leave lasting impact.

Our mission is to help our authors protect their soul's work, expand HER platform beyond the page, and turn HER message into a timeless legacy.

www.fempower.pub | @fempower.pub ⊙

www.ingramcontent.com/pod-product-compliance
Lightning Source LLC
Chambersburg PA
CBHW051305120626
46547CB00015B/2094